Cursed Karma of past life in Vedic Jyotisha

By - Hemant Bhatt

Cursed Karma of past life in Vedic Jyotisha

By - Hemant Bhatt

PARTRIDGE
A Penguin Random House Company

ISBN:	Softcover	978-1-4828-3407-9
	eBook	978-1-4828-3406-2

To order additional copies of this book, contact
Partridge India
000 800 10062 62
orders.india@partridgepublishing.com

www.partridgepublishing.com/india

CONTENTS

Preamble Notes

ॐ आदित्यम् गणनाथम् च देवीं रुद्रम् च केश्वम्। पंचदैवत्यमित्युक्तम् सर्व कर्मेषु पूजयेत्।

This book is based on traditional Vedic Astrology, the hora shastra. Many Sanskrit words and verses are taken here to give the base. Due to this spelling & grammatical tools in built in computer is of little help, room for proofing and editing; hope readers will take this in its true prospective.

There are many abbreviations used for names in Sanskrit such as Rashi, Planets, Stars viz. Pfalguni for Purvafalguni UFalguni for Uttrafalguni, etc. etc. In addition, divisional charts abbreviation is used sucha as Rasi chart as D1, navamsa chart as D9, 40th divisional chart [axavedamsa] as D40 etc etc.

There are many verses taken from Bruhat Parashara Hora Shastra popularly known as BPHS, Mumbai, and Khemraja Shrikrishnadas Hindi edition.

Except one or two charts selected here are of the natives known to author, seen them, their charts, and collected the briefs in person. There are many charts could not be coupled here as I do not want to creat voulume here but just try to say that in hora shastra also past life karma technique is given. There are many 'KarmaVipaaka' treaties available like KarmaVipakaSamhita and ViraSimhaavlokan Samhita where expiation is given for cursed karma of past life. In addition, there are 'Smrutis' [Hindu Law Book] available which especially deals with such cursed karma expiation methods. In hora shastra Yoga Jyotish is treated as separated branch and when this yoga is cancelled or vitiated otherwise is caused by cursed karma of past life.

This is my humble effort and prudent astrologers will carry on this quest. If time and lord permits me, will take Yoga Jyotish in light of past life karma in next volume of this book.

Chapter-01

Karma – Definition and its sources

Karma is to serve, to do, or to act. In a broad sense, put briefly, to do something with desire is karma. To do karma diligently, without expectations of its fruits and in equilibrium [with supreme soul of godhead] is akarma and to do sinful acts is vikarma. Vikarma may give rise to curse, Karma causes circumambulation of birth-rebirths and Akarma helps in achieving ultimate moksha.

There are many theories expounded in our Vedic literatures and Upanishads about karma and its nexus to birth and rebirth and the manner in which one get liberated from this process. In each Upanishad, Brahma Gyana is elaborated. One such is Shvetashvatara Upnishad. In Chapter-1, Stanza-6 [Shankar bhasya Gita Press], it is explained why our conditional soul is roaming in this cosmic world taking birth and rebirth through various wombs. I present this theory of karma in the following pages as per my humble knowledge and understanding of these scriptures.

The soul in the corporeal body [means destitute position of spirit or mind; something different from soul] in misconception believes it as super soul, roaming in various wombs such as humans, birds & animals, insects, reptiles etc. etc. as conditional soul. 'पृथगात्मानं प्रेरितारं च मत्वा ...pṛthagātmānaṁ preritāraṁ ca matvā' means conditional soul in corporeal body in misconception believes the stimulating supreme soul [Godhead] being different and separate form than its conditional soul, believes itself as super soul roaming in various wombs. 'अन्योऽसावन्योऽहमस्मि इतिजीवेश्वरभेद् दर्शनेन संसारे परिवर्तन इत्यर्थः ...anyo'sāvanyo'hamasmi itijīveśrvarabheda darśanena saṁsāre parivartana ityarthaḥ'

The stimulating supreme soul [Godhead] is different from my soul in my corporeal body, which is a separate form of conditional soul. In this manner when soul in corporeal body sees the piercing difference in Godhead, the conditional soul goes through circumambulation in various wombs. In addition, while roaming, this conditional soul of destitute mind and spirit does karma and vikarma [sinful things – paap/dusht karma] repeatedly, trapped in this vicious circle of birth and rebirth. Now, then the important thing is how the conditional soul begets moksha and the reply is that this happens when the conditional soul understands 'अहं ब्रह्मास्मि....ahaṁ brahmasmi' i.e. that godhead is inside me. Moreover, in contemplation visualises the supreme soul in deep concentration and with this help of the deep absorption and devotion to the supreme soul, the conditional soul is subdued and purified. Somewhere it resembles with 'यत् ब्रह्माण्डे तत् पिण्डे ... yat brahmāṇḍe tat piṇḍe' i.e. whatever is found in our universe here including the supreme soul also found inside the body i.e. the conditional soul.

In the same chapter-5, shloka-11, the manner in which karma leads the soul to births and rebirths is elaborated.

सङ्कल्पनस्पर्शनदृष्टिमोहैर्ग्रासाम्बुवृष्ट्याचात्मविवृद्धिजन्म।

कर्मानुगान्यनुक्रमेणदेहीस्थानेषुरूपाण्यभिसंप्रपध्यते॥ ....saṅkalpanasparśana dṛṣṭimohairgrāsāmbuvṛṣṭyācātmavivṛddhijanma | karmānugānyanukramenạdehī sthāneṣu rūpāṇyabhisaṁprapadhyate | |

I will try to explain the concept behind this shloka. The manner in which our corporeal body grows and develops with the intake of food-water-oxygen etc.; in the same way the karma performed by the conditional soul through desire [moha], will, persuasion or personification [sankalpa], sensation & feelings [sparsha] and intellectual observation [darshana] will result in re-birth in suitable form of womb according to these karma. In addition, conditional soul consumes the fruits of those karmas. First, our will or wish makes us eager to enjoy the senses of sight, sound, touch, taste etc, then comes the perception [darshana], which produces desire and that ultimately, pushes us to act or function karma. According to the ripening of this karma [KarmaVipaka], the conditional soul take the birth-rebirth in the form of male, female, impotent using various wombs of humans, celestial bodies, animals, birds, insects etc. etc. The conditional soul obtains the corporeal body and attains triguna prakruti according to its Karmas.

This entire law of karma is auto operative and nothing is spared. Let us simplify how the above system of karma works by an appropriate example. It is rather complex to assess the law of karma.

[01] You are hungry and wish to prepare and consume food – this is wish-feeling-impulse personified called Sankalpa. Our conscious and subconscious mind has

all feelings, emotions, desire, impulses which help identifies the nature of karma. This is the identification and interpretation phase.
[02] You prepare food – this is the sense of touch phase called Sparsh.
[03] You want to satiate this hunger so you prepared food– this is the perception phase called Darshana.
[04] You eat and feed the stomach to satisfy the hunger – this is the desire state called Moha.
The foregoing is the natural state of karma. Now, we will look at the complexity of this karma.
While eating, you see a street dog approaching you wagging its tail and you feed the dog - this is good and is rajas guna. But you are afraid the dog might spoil your food and you hit the dog and this is your tamas guna. But if you spare the food before you eat for dogs and insects then it is your satvik guna. All karmas of yours are sanchit karmas and will give its results at appropriate time. The karma rule is simple: if you hit the dog, then dog will bite you or you will suffer due to the dog and this is your prarabdha karma and cannot be changed. When you see the dog approaching, the impulse is recognised [sankalpa]. Your intelligent perception [darshan] conceived that it might spoil your food as you hate dogs or are afraid of dogs and you in trance [moha], decided to hit the dog, took the stick or stone or something in your hand [sparsha] and finally being a dog-hater, you hit the dog.

It is further said in the next Shloka of the same text that the conditional soul, the body bearer by the virtue of its punya/paapa karma, continuously takes the various bodily forms/ shapes of macro and micro bodies. Then karma and mental accomplishment of this bodily form work as merger and coincidence, the carnal cause [samyoga] of another body form-shape of the conditional soul is pursued.

There are many perceptions of karma found in our Vedic literature –net world and would like to reinstate some as under.

The law of karma explains why each individual has a unique mental disposition, a unique physical appearance, and unique experiences. These are the numerous and various effects of the countless actions, which each individual has performed in the past. We cannot find any two people who have created exactly the same history of actions throughout their past lives, and so we cannot find two people with identical states of mind, identical experiences, and identical physical appearances. Each person has a different individual karma. Some people enjoy good health while others are constantly ill. Some people are very beautiful while others are very ugly. Some people have a happy disposition that is easily pleased while others have a sour disposition and are rarely delighted by anything. Some people easily understand the meaning of spiritual teachings while others find them difficult and obscure. BPHS in its opening chapter treats this as three attributes-qualities namely, triguna prakruti 'tamas', 'rajas' and 'satva'.

"Karma" literally means "deed" or "act", and more broadly, means the natural justice of cause and effect, action and reaction, which Vedic Indian belief governs all consciousness. Karma is not fate [prarabdha] for we act with what can be described as a conditioned free will creating our own destinies. According to the Vedas, if we render goodness, we will reap goodness; if we render evil, we will reap evil reward. Karma refers to the totality of our actions and their concomitant reactions in this and previous lives, all of which determine our future. The conquest of karma lies in intelligent action and dispassionate reaction. Not all karmas rebound immediately. Some accumulate and return unexpectedly in this or other lifetimes. Human beings are said to produce karma in four ways and such sinful karmas are called multi fold paap karma.

* Manasik karma [or paap] - through thoughts, our ill thoughts

* Vachika karma [or paap] - through words, our ill words

* Kayika karma [or paap] - through our bodily actions that we perform ourselves

* Sansargika karma [or paap] - through actions others perform under our instructions or vice verse

This fifth one is the contribution of Kaliyuga, the modern era.

* Actions committed for material gratifications – arthika karma [or paap]; this may be a part of mansik, vachik, kayika and samsargika.

Everything that we have ever thought, spoken, done or caused is karma, as is also that which we think, speak or do this very moment. Hindu scriptures divide karma into three kinds as under.

* Sanchita is the accumulated karma. It would be impossible to experience and endure all karmas in one lifetime. From this stock of sanchita karma, a handful is taken out to serve one lifetime and this handful of actions, which have begun to bear fruit and which will be exhausted only on their fruit being enjoyed and not otherwise, is known as prarabdha karma.

* Prarabdha or Fruit-bearing karma is the portion of accumulated karma that has "ripened" and appears as a particular problem or soothing in the present life.

* Kriyamana is everything that we produce in the current life. All kriyamana karmas flow in to sanchita karma and consequently shape our future. Only in human life we can change our future destiny. After death we lose Kriya Shakti (ability to act) and do (kriyamana) karma until we are born again in another human body.

Actions performed consciously are weighted more heavily than those done unconsciously. On this basis some believe that only human beings who can distinguish right from wrong can do (kriyamana) karma. Therefore animals and young children are considered incapable of creating new karma (and thus cannot affect their future destinies) as they are incapable of discriminating between right and wrong. This view is explained by the concepts of a

Karma-deha ('action' body) and a Bhoga-deha ('completion' body).

Our destiny was shaped long before the body came into being. As long as the stock of sanchita karma lasts, a part of it continues to be taken out as prarabdha karma for being enjoyed in one lifetime, leading to the cycle of birth and death. A Jiva cannot attain moksha (liberation) from the cycle of birth and death, until the accumulated sanchita karmas are completely exhausted. It can be lasted only when we do proper karma 'akarma'. The cycle of birth and death on earth is formed from 8.4 million forms of life, only one of which is human. Only humans are in position to do something about our destiny by doing the right thing at the right time. Through positive actions, pure thoughts, prayer, mantras and meditation, we can resolve the influence of karma in the present life and turn our destiny for the better. A spiritual master knowing the sequence in which our karma will bear fruit can help us. As humans, we have the opportunity to speed up our spiritual progress with the practice of good karma. We produce negative karma because we lack knowledge and clarity.

Unkindness yields spoiled fruits, called paap, and good deeds bring forth sweet fruits, called punya. As one acts, so does one become: one becomes virtuous by virtuous action, and evil-by-evil action.

Karma means not only action, but also the result of an action is one view and what is stored is sanchita and result is prarabdha. Whatever we are going through now is the result of previous actions and desires of usage of free will of mind, not just of this life, but many lives.

Karma is the sum total of our actions both in this life and in the preceding lives, every action, reaction and rewards are auto operative and humans have virtually no control over that at least for the common person. According to the theory of Vedic dharma shastra theory, one will not cease to exist after death, only body that dies, and the astral body [the soul spirit] and causal body [source of the body existing with the universal impersonal spirit] continue the quest to find another body according to its karma. The causal body has all our Karmas stored in it as seeds, seeds that result in rebirth. As long as man has not exhausted all his Karmas, he has to be born again. All our actions and thoughts become the seeds for our future lives. Karma is at the root of this cycle of births and deaths. Repeatedly Karma makes us take birth. Countless times have we been born and countless times have we died.

Vedic Jyotish is the primary occult science to see the karma of the native and is stated therein BPHS as under.

अहोरात्रस्य पूर्वान्त्यलोपाद्‌ होराऽवशिष्यते । तस्य विज्ञानमात्रेण जातकर्मफलं

वदेत्‌ ॥

Ahorātrasyapūrvāntyalopādorā'vaśiṣyate I tasyavijñāna

mātreṇa ātakarmaphalaṃ vadet II

The word Hora is derived from Ahoratr after dropping the first and last syllables. Thus, Hora (Lagnas) remains in between Ahoratr (i.e. day and night) and after knowing this Hora shastra the results of the karma of the native can be best known.

अधुना संप्रवक्ष्यामि तन्वारूढफ़लं द्विज । यस्य ज्ञानमात्रेण जायते कर्मसूचकः ॥

adhunāsaṃpravakṣyāmianvārūḍhaphalaṃ dvija । yasya jñānamātreṇa jāyate karmasūcakaḥ ॥

Oh! Dwija, now I foretell the results of ascendant elevated [Arudha pada of Ascendant] and its knowledge is indicative of the karma [of the native].

अधुना संप्रवक्ष्याम्युपपदं च द्विजोत्तम । यस्य विज्ञानमात्रेण जायते [कर्म] फ़लसूचकः ॥

adhunā saṃpravakṣyāmyupapadaṃ ca dvijottama ।

yasya vijñānamātreṇa jāyate [karma] phalasūcakaḥ ॥

In this upapada arudha the sage told the same thing as in arudha lagna verse, but with different wordings only and we have to construe it in its true manner as hora shastra itself is 'falit shastra' so what is said is 'karmasuchakaH' as per my understanding.

मिश्रे मिश्रा मृतिरिति एवं कर्माणि विप्र भोः । कर्मभावे विशेषेण फ़लदाता द्विजोत्तम ॥

miśre miśrā mṛtiriti evaṃ karmāṇi vipra bhoḥ I

karmabhāve viśeṣeṇa phaladātā dvijottama II

In this manner [in the context of 3H]; mixture of planets causes the death according to the karma of the native. Oh! Excellent Brahmin especially this abstract contemplation of karma [karmabhava or karmayoga] is result giver.

As per Bruhat Jataka of Shri Varahamihira in the first chapter verse-3, it is said that the astrology is the science called Hora Shastra from the compounding of two words of Aho and Ratri and its speaks of the results of the good and bad deeds done by the men in their previous births.

With the help of stars, planets, houses and sign significations, attributes and dictum of this science of Vedic astrology [Horashastra], by deep study, concentration and soul meditation we can conclude the karma of the native. However, very few can do that and those who are appropriate [aatmasaat] to do this are real sages, the omniscient.

Chapter – 02

Definition and source of curse

Curse is known as ‘shaapa’ in Sanskrit and to construe its lexicon we have to go to its Vedic literature understanding and relevance. Curse is raised thru live beings such as humans, serpents, sages, etc. and in our Vedic literature also thru’ Lords [Devas-Devis], Gandharvas, Pitrus etc. and is laid upon humans is our subject matter resolved by sage Shri Parashara in his treaty BPHS.

Definition:

When a native constantly or extremely does distress, harm or sufferings, agony, agitate, unsocial-uncultured-immoral things, broken promises, and clever [दुष्कर्म] things to abuse other living beings. It is done in such way that the soul of that particular live being becomes perplex and restless. As a result it is physically dead or is not able to live normally and has to suffer for its life time; then the lamented soul sighs,[निःश्वास] thinks and or speaks inauspicious or harmful for the native and this is curse.

The curse would affect according to the predominant degree of the wrongdoing and according to the atmabala, karma and tapobala of the soul and native. In our Puranas we find many story related to various curses of humans, serpents, Gandharvas, Devas, Devis etc. etc. and is the true base to give us the clues of sufferings and root cause of curse and this can be seen from the natives chart as suggested by the Sage ShriParashara. Lords are known as super soul living inside us and are living beings as 'sagunasvarupa' as per our Vedic literature.

For e.g. in Shir Satyanarayana Vrata Katha, lord gives curse to Sadhu Vanik for his unsocial and untrue conduct coupled with non-performance of Vrata and in result Sadhu is imprisoned and his family loses everything and is starved for food. The very important thing behind our Puranas is that it gives us the way of life and moksha, the only thing required is the real literal understanding and vision of it. When we understand it we will realize that the curse does not arise normally and if it arises then it is something that has to be consumed and there is no way out unless and until you get the serenity [Prashannata] of the lord concerned which is not easy as correct guidelines are required. 'Pitrus' are also known as lord in our Vedic literature called 'pitru deva', similarly 'nagadevata'. Even in our Vedic literature 'atithi' i.e. unknown guest is termed lord as 'atithi deva'. Whenever curse is arising, it will hit the chart and the native accordingly, has to suffer with heart wailing pain. Why this Sadhu Vanikis cursed by lord Shri Satyanarayana in the guise of 'Dandi' and why were the karma so bad that they turned into curse. I have taken this Satyanarayana Katha as it is very popular and admired for its rewards but seldom had we made souls think of it. This Katha is depicted in SkandaPurana.
Following are the karma accumulated and turned into curse to Sadhu Vanik.
[01] Sadhu just determined to do the vrata only if he will get child i.e. he keeps 'badha' in hindi it is called 'manauti'; gain seeking perception.

[02] On getting child, did not do Vrata and postponed it; future perception & promise; broken promise. Promise to do something or to perform arises from pure & pious heart and when it is broken serenity of soulis impeded and curse rises. In our vedic culture Atma [soul] is Parmatma [lord] and if we cheat our soul we have to suffer as if we cheat our own GOD! This is the curse for broken promise.
[03] On another occasion also, he did not do the Vrata; earned with unethical ways, became ill natured; practical perception brings materialness.
[04] Got punishments of imprisonment and loss of wealth and by virtue of blessings of lord worshipped by wife again got the materialness i.e. wealth.
[05] Again Sadhu disregarded lord in guise of dandi [sagunasvarupa] and is at verge of losing every thing.He becomes careless and leering on Dandi.
Here it is said that the loss [becomes wealth less] is incurred due to the curse of the Dandi. Here it is the shaapa of Deva in guise of Dandi i.e. Sanyasi Brahmin, indicated as Brahma Shaapa in Bruhat Parashar Hora Shastra. In normal conditions curse does not arise, however, how curse arises is very well depicted as above; its silent features are as under:
[01] Sadhu merchant earned a lot and is intoxicated by it as his wealth is not pure i.e. earned by wrong means and without labour as king gifted him [depicted in the end of chapter-3 of Satyanaryana Katha];
[02] Sadhu is overconfident and neither respected the lord but leered at lord. This is very important that if we cannot serve we should respect the lord and not leer;

[03] Sadhu lied to the lord. To lie or to harm others can be construed here. These factors together will produce the curse; the degree of predominance may differ.

Here the real work of astrologers starts, as he has to see the karma of native for which he is suffering and unless and until astrologer cannot do that, he is trapped in the vicious cycle of material perception i.e. 'vyavahaarabuddhi'. For which karma native is suffering is secreted in natal chart in the form of signs and planets and to read it and render correct guideline is astrologers' true duty.

अहोरात्रद्यंतलोपाद्धोरेति प्रोच्यते बुधैः। तस्य हि ज्ञानमात्रेण जातकर्मफ़लं वदेत्॥ ch-3, Part-1, ०२॥ [BPHS – Khemraj Mumbai edition]

ahorātradyaṁtalopāddhoreti procyate budhaiḥ | tasya hi jñānamātreṇa jātakarmafalaṁ vadet | | 02 | |

Surmise meaning is from the word 'Ahoratra' first alphabet 'A' and last one 'tra' is dropped to form another word 'Hora' the subject matter of predictive astrology and that subject is to foretell-recognize the karma of the native.

According to Saravali the classical treaty of Vedic astrology ch.-2, the Horāśāstra is indicative of effects of one's Karma.

Opening chapter of 'Jataka Shara Deepa' as per verse 6 it is said that good or bad or the mixed results are to be ascertained by a native according to the karma done in the past life of native and Hora shastra enlightens this by what is depicted in natal chart.

प्राग्जन्मकर्मसदसत्फ़लपाक शस्तिः। होराप्रकाशयति तामिह वर्णपंक्तिं॥ ०६॥

prāgjanmakarmasadasatfalapāka śastiḥ | horāprakāśayati tāmiha varṇapaṁktiṁ | | 06 | |

In the same text in the same chapter at verse, 36 it is depicted that by doing propitiation, expiation [prayaschit], charities, etc. as told in the 'karamavipaaka' even the good results may not be emerged. Then in such occasion, this should be done two or three times with lots of efforts then only desired results will surely be obtained.

There are too many examples of curses in our Puranas and the way out is either to take the serenity of that particular living being or to purify your karma. Basically one's karma is the root cause of one's suffering according to the predominance of bad or worse karma and curse arises when karma is constant and extreme at worst degree.

Let us see Padma Purana where in Part-4 BramhaKhanda Chapter-26 how broken promises forms the curse is very well said and worth noting. In the same purana and part in chapter-5 the reasons for childlessness in the form of curse is given which I would like to surmise as under and how it is forming part of BPHS. Remedial measures are also given *vis-a-vis* shaapa.

[01] The native in his previous adobe if takes away the source of income or wealth of Brahman thru other, then, the native will be childless in the current birth era. If the native with deep faith listen the puranas and donate land with grain crops on it, gold idol of cow or living milky cow with Daxina and gold idol of Ista Deva then the birth of child is sure in current birth era.

This remedial measure is to be performed prudently according to the time, regional customs, culture and economic condition of the native. If we give our one room with free meals or piece of land rent-free for eleven months lease is equivalent to the donation of land with crop; or according to the economic condition one may donate some grains with Daxina as token for land. To listen to cited puranas has special reference here, as it is the 'Shruti Vakya' that 'श्रुतं हरति पापानि ...śrutaṁ harati pāpāni' i.e. by listening puranas and vedic literature our worst-papa karma diluted-evaporates if we make the soul think and we find the way of expiation thru that. To donate cow means either you donate token money for that or silver idol if cannot make gold cow, or the best way is to serve the live cow especially with calf. To serve the cow is just an instance and is relevant to every live being especially old and a helpless human, which is a true, sense of our puranas and is to be construed accordingly. If we take our puranas with this kind of Vedic literature understanding, then only we can do expiation and thereby we can dilute our curse and get the desired results.

According to BPHS, how we can see the above karma of taking away the sources of income or wealth of Brahman etc. and how this resulted in the curse for childlessness is well narrated as per the verses below. BPHS, P-I, Chpter-28, verse-8 [Mumbai Khemraj Edition]

मेषेमेषनवांशकेषु........ ब्रूयाद्विप्रधनं मीने पूर्वार्धे तु विपश्चितः। उतरार्धे धनादानं तद्वधं परिकल्पितम्॥

।meṣe meṣanavāṁśakeṣu.....brūyādvipradhanaṁ mīne pūrvārdhe tu vipaśrvitaḥ ।utarārdhe dhanādānaṁ tadvadhaṁ parikalpitam ।।

In Mesha Rashi, Mesha navamsa [in Aries ascendant Aries division nine] and onward the karma of previous birth of the native is seen and accordingly in first part of Meena navamsa [Taurus ascendant] the source of income of Brahman and in second part of the Meena navamsa taking away the wealth of Brahman.
Sage Shri Parahsara is the father of sage Shri VedaVyasa the creator of our eighteen puranas. Father [Parashar] the creator of Vedic astrology and son [Vedvyasa] is of Puranas see the nexus.
The karma narrated as in 'padmapurana' below is of prenatal adobe and result was consumed due to that in the next birth.
[02] If a female native does harm to the others child or murders or cause to do so in her previous adobe then she will be childless in current birth. If the female native donates gold idol of cow to Brahmana with deep faith and before donation wash the holy feet of Brahman and religiously drink that water, then listen to 'Padma Purana', donate gold idol [of Vishnu] with plenty of money as Daxina to Brahman then that female will have child in the current birth era.
To wash the feet and to drink that water has to be understood properly. This simply means to serve Brahman. Brahman can be anyone if we take 'Brahman by karma theory' means a person who is engaged in the true development of society and religion to maintain peace and welfare. It also means to serve Brahman who is in need such as very poor and old or is ailed with dreadful disease etc.
Pisces ascendant and Pisces navamsa or Libra sign and Gemini navamsa is the configuration to see in the chart.

[03] The native who did not save after seeing the drowning child in water, the native will be childless.
Donation of bullock with gold, banana and clothes, penance to please good children, donate virgin girl for marriage to Brahman [kanyadaana], listen Padma Purana prescribed here for childbirth.
Scorpio ascendant and Pisces navamsa is the combo to see in the chart.

[04] The native who expulses [निराश .. nirāśa] or disappoints 'atithi' i.e. unknown guest and angered upon that 'atithi' and penalised him without any cause then the native will be childless.
If the native gives respect and propitiate Brahamana and 'atithi' and donates water and food and build or cause to build best Temple, the native will be bestowed with child.
Cancer ascendant and Pisces navamsa is to see in the chart or Gemini sign and Gemini navamsa.
[05] The native kills the premature Garbha [conception-foetus- embryo] of the other; the progeny [child] of that native will be destroyed or dead.
If the native observes the Vrata of 'Ekadashi' with spouse then will be bestowed with children and spouse for lifetime.
Libra ascendant and Pisces navamsa
[06] If the 'shudra' [lower caste by karma] does harm to the cow and or bullock; or if the native rapes, molests, takes away, or kidnaps Brahman female, he will become impotentor nincompoop.
Shudra means the person with bad karma and Brahman female means holy, pious and virgin females and best word is 'dharma parayana – patiprayanana' i.e. those

feminine devoted to fidelity religiously and their husband.

For the expiation of this karma, the native must do some pious and holy deeds and on that account will be born as a female.

Virgo ascendant and Pisces navamsa is to see here.

[07] If the native kills or causes death of the children of a Brahman, then up to seven births, the cruel child will take birth.

Aries ascendant Scorpio navamsa is to see.

I am giving you the six verses of Padma Purana wherein these curses are given; Part-4 BramhaKhanda Chapter-05.

पूर्व जनम्नि यो मर्त्यो वर्तन्रं ब्राह्मणस्य च। हरेद्वाहरयेदत्र पुत्रहिनोभवेत्किल॥७॥ पूर्व जनम्नि या नारी परबालकघातनं। करोतिकपटेनैव बालहीनाभवेद् ध्रुवं ॥१०॥ जलेनिमग्नं बालं यो दृष्ट्वा या न समुद्धरेत्। इहजन्मन्य पुत्रोवैसाऽपुत्रीचभवेद् ध्रुवं॥१३॥ पूर्वजनमनियोमर्त्यो निराशंचातिथिंद्विज। कुरयात्क्रोधेनदंडंच पुत्रहीनोभवेद् ध्रुवम्॥१६॥ पूर्वजनमनियानारी भ्रूणहत्यांचयोनरः। कुर्यात्सामृतवत्साच मृतवत्सोभवेद् ध्रुवं ॥१८॥ पूर्वजनमनियोमूढोब्रह्मबालकघातकः। तस्यक्रूरोभवेत्पुत्रः सप्तजन्मान्तरौद्विजः॥३८॥

pūrva janamni yo martyo vartanraṁ brāhmaṇasya ca | haredvāharayedatra putrahinobhavetkila ||7|| pūrva janamni yā nārī parabālakaghātanaṁ| karotikapaṭenaiva bālahīnābhaved dhruvaṁ ||8|| jalenimagnaṁ bālaṁ yo dṛṣṭvā yā na samuddharet| ihajanmanya putrovaisā'putrīcabhaved dhruvaṁ

।।13।।pūrvajanamaniyomartyo nirāśaṁcātithiṁdvija। kurayātkrodhenadaṁḍaṁca putrahīnobhaved dhruvam ।।16।। pūrvajanamaniyānārī bhrūṇahatyāṁcayonaraḥ। kuryātsāmṛtavatsāca mṛtavatsobhaved dhruvaṁ ।।18।। pūrvajanamaniyomūḍhobrahmabālakaghātakaḥ। tasyakrūrobhavetputraḥ saptajanmāntaraudvijaḥ ।।38।।

Therefore, the main source of curse is the KARMA of native that is harmful to other live being or self-destroying in any way. The nature of Dharma is so micro that it is difficult to decide which karma is harmful, which is not, and we will not go deep into that decision, as our subject matter is rise from curse and suffering of the native and its remedial measures.

Chapter- 03

Curse & Karma in Vedic Astrology

Curse:
In BPHS, a detailed outlook of curse is given in independent chapter. First, the sage has given preamble as to how to look at curse with respect to all the twelve bhava and how it arises.
The verses given here under are taken from Khemraj Krishanadas Mumbai edition.

पार्वत्युवाच

देवदेवजगन्नाथशूलपाणेवृषध्वज। केनयोगेनमर्त्यानांजायतेशिशुनाशनं । ०१।

तत्सर्वमत्रयोगेनब्रूहिमेशशिशेखर। शापमोक्षं चकृपयाप्राणिनामल्पमेधसाम्।

०२।

शङ्करउवाच -

साधुपुष्टंत्वयादेविकथयामिसविस्तरात्। श्रृणुष्वैकमनाभूत्वाबलाबलवशादपि ।

०३ ।

ज्ञेयंसुनिश्चितंसर्वंराशिचक्रेविषेशतः। मेषादिमीनपर्यन्तंमूर्त्यादिद्वादशक्रमात्

।०४।

भावं च भावजंज्ञात्वाफलंब्रूयाद्विचक्षणः। तनुर्वित्तंबन्धुमातृपुत्रशत्रुस्मरोमृतिः।

०५।

पितृकर्मचलाभं च व्ययांताभावसंज्ञकाः। ०६ १/२ ।

Pārvatyuvāca

devadevajagannāthaśūlapāṇevṛṣadhvaja ।
kenayogenamartyānāṃjāyateśiśunāśanaṃ । 01 ।
tatsarvamatrayogenabrūhi me śaśiśekhara । śāpamokṣaṃ ca kṛpayāprāṇināmalpamedhasām । 02 । śaṅkara uvāca - sādhupuṣṭaṃtvayādevikathayāmisavistarāt ।
śṛṇuṣvaikamanābhūtvābalābalavaśādapi ।03 ।
jñeyaṃsuniśrcitaṃsarvaṃrāśicakreviṣeśataḥ ।
meṣādimīnaparyantaṃmūrtyādidvādaśakramāt ।04 । bhāvaṃ ca bhāvajaṃjñātvāphalaṃbrūyādvicakṣaṇaḥ ।
tanurvittaṃbandhumātṛputraśatrusmaromṛtiḥ । 05 ।pitṛkarmaca lābhaṃ ca vyayāṃtābhāvasaṃjñakāḥ । 06 1/2 ।

Meaning -

Goddess mother Parvati asked [to lord Shiva] –
Oh! Lord of the lord Mahadeva, the universe lord with spear in hand and bull sign [or a virtuous lord, वृषध्वज...Vṛṣadhvaja], on account of which combinations, childlessnes or destructions of child is occured for humans. Oh! Lord Shashishekhara please tell me all these combinations [yogas] and how ignorant [dull-witted – अल्पमेधस् ... alpamedhas] living beings [humans] can liberate - release such curses.

Lord Shri Shankara speaks –
Great! This is the thriving question, I am to tell you the complete detailed reply, and you [please] listen to it with full concentration i.e. attentive mind. All these are [curse combinations] firmly resolved distinctively in the natal chart [of the native concerned] i.e. Rashi Chakra i.e.

zodiac chart [of twelve signs, houses and planets] according to its relative strength. Embodiment of this zodiac or natal chart is in the form of Mesh [Aries] to Meena [Pisces] twelve signs respectively. The house, house lord and karaka [भावं च भावजं] be construed intelligently and foretold the curse combinations cleverly-wisely. These twelve bhavas i.e. houses forms are 1H-self physique, 2H- wealth, 3H- brothers-sisters, 4H- mother, 5H – son, 6H- enemy, 7H- sexual love, 8H- death, 9H- father, 10H- karma, 11H- gain and 12H- separation or loss.

Preamble Notes -

The important point is the word 'शिशुनाशनं..śiśunāśanaṃ' used by the sage indicating child destructionis irrespective of its gender and confirms that the house of child is the house of live birth of child, male or female, though it is indicated as 'house of son' many times.

Here it is clear that the child destruction or childlessness is occurred due to inauspicious combinations of planets, signs and houses. This inauspicious yoga is then referred to as Shaapa i.e. curse in the second stanza. Important question that arises here is what iscurse and how it isformed. Our general knowledge says that curse arises through bad karmas and bad karmas are reflected as various combinations of planets in houses and signs. It is many times at various places said in BPHS that this Vedic astrology is the science of seeing karma of the native and if inauspicious yoga are formed in the chart, it can easily be construed as bad karma of the native that curse childlessness or destruction thereof. This is the reason why bad yoga is the result of bad karma, which in turn referred to as curse of childlessness or destruction of child. So it is better we understand this curse concept vis-a-vis karma of the native in previous-current birth reflected by some bad yoga in the natal chart i.e. rasichakra. In kaliyuga you have to pay for all your karma of current birth era in the same current birth era and only if there is nothing left of the previous birth karma, then there will be moksha, but this is other school or part so we will not debate on it. There are various kind of curses depicted in the chart with respect of father, mother, spouse etc. related to child destruction or childlessness. The curse is depicted for childlessness primarily 5H as known and is formatted by respective house of father, mother, spouse etc. to start with. And we can take it over to other houses like wealth less or destruction of wealth [2H], spouseless [7H], without job or occupation [6-10-7H] so on and so forth for all the twelve houses of the zodiac chart we can discern the curses with respect to curse of father, mother, brother etc. etc. Sample list is as under and professional astrologer can add as many as per their prudence and expertise as per significations of houses and its karakas.

H with other factors	Effects due to various curse of father, mother, brother etc.
1H	Physically handicapped or sever defect, genetic or post diseases or accidental effects, mental-physical retard making devoid of every happiness etc.
2H	Wealthless or destruction of wealth, family,

	dumbness etc
3H	Brotherless, deaf, earless , sever cowardice, motionless, premature death,etc
4H	Home or houseless, academicless, motherless, etc.
5H	Childlessness, wisdomless
6H	Joblessness, severe diseases, maternal uncle less
7H	no spouse or spouse destruction, no conception or loss of conception,impotency
8H	Frequent Rapes or forceful sex, constant cutthroat debt, suicidal attempts, etc.
9H	Wicked and impiousness, aimlessness, without limbs
10H	no knight and award or loss of it, occupation-joblessness, no father or destruction of father
11H	Without wife & children, friendlessness
12 H	excessive expenditure, sleeplessness, severe intoxication, unsocial-illicit sex etc

In this manner from the house [bhava], house lord &karakas [bhavajam] for all the above twelve house we can derive curses as per cleverness, intelligence and wisdom. All these are [curse combinations] firmly resolved distinctively in the natal chart [of the native concerned] i.e. Rashi Chakra i.e. zodiac chart [of twelve signs, houses and planets] as depicted above according to its relative strength. This is very important that the sage suggests importance of relative strength of planets; without proper evaluation of strength in the terms of shadabala, avastha, conjunction etc. curse cannot be predicted.

गुरुर्लग्नेश दारेश पुत्रस्थानाधिपेशु च । ६ १/२ ।

सर्वेषु बलहीनेषु वक्तव्या त्वनपत्यता। रव्याररराहुशनयः पुत्रस्थाबलसंयुताः । ७।

कारकाद्यात्क्षीणबलात् अनपत्यत्वमादिषेत् । ८ १/२ ।

Gururlagneśadāreśaputrasthānādhipeśu ca । 6 1/2 ।

sarveṣubalahīneṣuvaktavyātvanapatyatā।ravyārarāhuśa

nayaḥputrasthābalasaṃyutāḥ।7।

kārakādyātkṣīṇabalātanapatyatvamādiṣet। 8 1/2 ।

Meaning:

Jupiter, Ascendant and its lord, 7H and its Lord and 5H and its lord of sudarshan chakra and Jupiter and 5th from 5H is 9H and its lord when ALL are weak or without strength childlessness is foretold. Sun, Mars, Rahu and Saturn posited with strength in the house of child and when karakas of child are powerless, childlessness can be foreseen.

Preamble Notes -

The word used is 'putrasthanaadhipeshu' which popularly known as 5H and includes 9H 5th from 5H from Ascendant, Moon, Sun and Jupiter. Jupiter is karaka of Child as 5H and 9H being lord of natural zodiac chart Sagittarius. In the same manner Sun is also karaka of child as lord natural zodiac chart sign Leo. Sun, Mars [destroying], Saturn and Rahu having separating elements are considered bad in house of child if they are strong and if karakas [Jupiter-Sun] are weak it causes childlessness.

These are the most important verses sage is giving to construe the basics of house of child, karakas of child and conception house. Let us understand the governance of child according to BPHS as under.

Jupiter: It is karaka of Child and 5H & 9H from Jupiter is 'putrasthana' i.e. house of child.

Ascendant: Ascendant and its lord is having general happiness in every respect and have a say in everything and is thus important. Also ascendant is 7th from 7H and is thus important for conception and happiness of child.

7th house: 7H and its lord are important for conception and given importance by the sage in the right consideration.

Putrashtana i.e. House/s of child: It is noteworthy that house of child is the live birth of conception i.e. gain of conception means 11H from 7th the house of conception; and similarly 11H from 1st house as per bhavatbhavam rule. So, 5H and 11H are house of child being live birth of conception. For destruction or loss of conception or no live birth to conception is 12H or 6H being 6th and 12th from 7H and 1H. 9H is also house of child being 5th from 5H and 11th from 11H.

7H i.e. house of conception: 7H is the house of conception and is pivotal being house of transfer of sperms from male to female to fertile the conception in result. If this house is not strong there, will be no conception and in result no child; even there will be no spouse then no child as a result. Gain of conception is live birth is stated above. The sage established the nexus of 7H and 5H.

Sarveshu Balahineshu i.e. destitute of strength or weak: it is suggested by Sage that all the above factors Jupiter [Karaka] , Ascendant [overall factor], 7H and house of child when weak childlessness exists.
Following are few factors that cause the planet weak.
[01] Planet in inimical sign, in duhasthana, combustion, betwixt two malefic, debilitated or with debilitated not cancelled etc. This is known as 'DuhasthaGraha', 'PiditGraha', 'GrasitGraha' [by nodes], 'paapakaratari' etc.
[02] Planet in trik sign, house, or its nakshatra conjunction
[03] Weak in shadabala, avastha and in navamsha
[04] Weak in basic avastha i.e. age, alertness, mood, activity etc.
[05] It is in relation with inimical and or malefic planets by aspect or conjunction.

Dire Malefic in House of child: Sun, Mars, Saturn and Rahu are dire malefic and if abide in house of child is separating [Sun-Saturn-Rahu] or destroying-extinction [Mars-Ketu] and if karaka of child is also in poor-worn away strength then childlessness is seen. HERE IT is noteworthy that four malefics are required to be in relation to cause childlessness or destruction of child. So, to cause curse more than two malefic [natural-functional] are required to be in relation to house of child and at the same time karaka in poor strength.

Karaka of child: karaka of child are Jupiter as natural karaka and natural zodiac 9H Sagittarius sign lord and Sun being natural zodiac 5H Leo sign lord.

Chara Karaka: Jupiter is fixed karaka of child and unfixed karaka is 'putrakaraka' as said in karakamsha chapter of BPHS.

Arudha and Upapada: Again, what is seen from sudarshan chakra for child is also seen from house of child of ArudhaLagna as per following verse of BPHS.

एवंलग्नपदाद्विप्रपुत्रभावादिचिन्तयेत॥ अ-१२ पुर्वखण्डश्लोक ३६ ॥

evaṃlagnapadādvipraputrabhāvādicintayeta ||

Also from upapada childlessness is seen as per the following verses of ch.12 part-I of BPHS.

लग्नादुपपदद्वापि योःराशिः सप्तमो द्विज। तन्नवांशा राशयोंशाः स्वसप्तमतदंशकाः।

तत्र पापे स्थिते दृष्टे उक्तफ़लं विदुः॥ २७॥ शनिः शुक्रस्तथा चान्द्रिः सप्तमांशग्रहेषु च।

त्रियोगकृते विप्र अपत्यरहितो नरः॥ २८॥

lagnādupapadadvāpi yoḥrāśiḥ saptamo dvija | tannavāṁśā rāśayoṁśāḥ svasaptamatadaṁśakāḥ | tatra pāpe sthite dṛṣṭe uktafalaṁ viduḥ | | 27 | | śaniḥ śukrastathā cāndriḥ saptamāṁśagraheṣu ca | triyogakṛte vipra apatyarahito naraḥ | | 28 | |

7H from LagnaArudha and Upapada and its navamsha and 7H of that navmsha if posited or aspected by malefic then above results will be gained [with respect to spouse]. [27]

On the same line, sage gives the analogy for child from 7H navamsa of Arudha and Upapada in verse 28 hereunder.

Triplicate yoga formed by 7H from LagnaArudha and or Upapada and its navamsha and 7H of that navmsha [or 9H] if posited [or aspected] by Saturn, Venus and Mercury childlessness is caused. [28]
Here very important resolution is given to see childlessness from Arudha, Upapada and navamsa of 7H. Many astrologers try to see this analogy from 9H of navamsa of 7H and consider the aspect of Saturn, Venus and Mercury if not posited in those houses. We should read stanza 27-28 conjointly as here lagnaarudha, upapada, and navamsa of 7H are considered for the result of 7H for progeny.
This chapter of Arudha and Upapada is important as it indicates the source of sufferings to discern the curses to some extent.

A planet causing the type of curse is as under.

Planets	Source of curse	Remarks
Rahu	Serpent – Sapa or Naga	Includes harm to-destruction of sapa or death on a/c of snake bite.
Sun	Father or its ancestors of direct lineage	Harm or non-services to them
Moon	Mother or its ancestors of direct lineage	Harm or non-services to them
Mars	Brothers or its ancestors of direct lineage	Harm or non-services to them
Mercury	Matul or maternal	Harm or non-services

	uncle or its ancestors of direct lineage	to them
Jupiter	Lord, Brahman, sage etc wise elders	Harm or non-services to them or broken promises
Venus	Wife or mistress or female in such relations	Harm or non-services to them or broken promises
Saturn	Preta	Harm or non-services to them or broken promises to any live being and after death could not attain PitruLoka

Ketu is not indicated to cause any curse specifically but can be construed that it is primarily concerned with serpent curse and its role is complex and multidimensional for other curses or act like auto–catalyst.

Karma:
Karma is an ocean with perpetual flow and we are mostly unaware of its final output to undergo as a result. The nature of law of karma can be stated as under.

- Law of wish & caution
- Law of action and reaction resulting from wish & caution
- Law of considerate reward due to action-reaction
- Law of punishment i.e. retribution

- Law of impression i.e. qualitative disposal

The wish and caution is the logical order of our deeds i.e. functions, keeps up our inner harmony. This law is immutable and inexorable and is perpetual in nature for lifetime and in broader sense for universe to exist. There are good and bad cautions or wishes, which resulted in action-reaction. First it rises to mental plane and functions in physical form to complete the karma i.e. implementation. If one causes sufferings and troubles to other, the native will in turn get the misery and pain. The law operates with scientific accuracy and meticulousness that means what you did you will get the same in unceasing precision. The law of considerate reward i.e. compensation keeps the balance and harmony in nature and the native in particular. The rule of natural justice is the result of this law, if you do evils you are to earn bad fruit to reap for you. Then comes the law of punishment and it operates both on mental and physical, or material or live plane. One cannot cheat another unless he cheats himself and one cannot hurt another unless he hurts himself and the working efficacy of this law of punishment of evils is like a two-way sword. When you chaet other, first you cheat your heart and parmamtma [lord] is in your heart, so, you first cheat your God. The law of impression operates in perpetual form carrying from birth to birth with inner soul represented in physical plane. When the native does something either good or bad some short of impression is created in mind; this also operates in the same manner when we listen and give soul-thinking, implementation to some Vedic literature and good things, which we call Samskara. These Samshkara in accession together forms the inner and outer behaviour of the native and are developed into habits which inbuilt the character of the native. This is known as qualitative disposal.

All these wishes, actions-reactions, compensation, punishment and character initiated from our Indriyas i.e. sensory organs, popularly known as Shadripus in Vedic literature, when restricted or controlled it turned to six strengths known as Shad Sampat. The soul is inbuilt in physique with Indriya saving its relation, the native does karma for soul and soul spontaneously inspires the native to do karma according to internal and external, present and past circumferences. This embodiment of karma is divided in three categories.
[01] Sanchit karma is past life karmas for which we have no control and we carry forward it.
[02] Prarabdha Karma is the fruitarian of past karmas for which our soul rested in present physique and endeavour pleasures and sufferings.
[03] Kriyamaan Karma is what we are to do or what we are doing. This will help us in forming our present and future means improve or injure it; this entails us to either improve or rectify or balance or worsen our past.

When astrologer reads the chart of the native,he should segregate these Sanchita Karma, Prarbdha Karma and Kriyaman karma. It is utmost important to know how we should know and assess the karmic profile of the native from birth chart. Sanchit and Prarbdha Karma is like inevitable and invisible imprint of life and we only have the scope for maneuvering the Kriyaman Karma either to improve or injure the future or improve or balance the past.

When we are alive in our body, mind and soul are united together, but as soon as we are dead, our body is turned into a corpse, mind becomes formless and soul is isolated. This isolated soul and mind formless, emotional and cognitive state searches for a soul as per the destined karma i.e. Prarabdha Karma. This initiated search of soul is completed when the body fit to its Prarabdha Karma is found and the transforming process of soul to body is started and that is what we call the ascendant, nadi, or precise division. The natural zodiac Aries sign and causal-manifested Ascendant or Nadi or Divisional sign governs this. Moon and Cancer or causal moon sign govern the formless and stateless emotional-cognitive mind moistened inside the body. Now body transformed, mind placed, so Soul rides on this consciousness and when the process is completed is known as birth in present. Sun and Leo or causal sun sign govern this soul manifestation. Prarabdha Karma destines this and everything from conception to birth to complete life cycle goes on accordingly. The natal chart is the map of Prarabdha i.e. destiny operative in the present given birth era. So the soul came with Sanchit Karma [purvapunya Sun or Leo or 5H] and its fruit is Prarbdha governed by 9H or Jupiter or Sagittarius sign. This may be the logic to vouch 9H for past birth and its sanchit karma the Sun or Atmakaraka and or most afflicted nakshatra-planet-sign-bhava for respective sufferings. This 9H is house of fortune is highly valued for its positive and pious vibrations. 9H is the 5th from 5H as per bhavatbhavam dictum and indicates the fruit i.e. Prarabdha of past birth/s. similarly, 5H is 9th from 9H and is deciding the available fruits of Sanchit Karma [5H] realized. Simple example of malefic in 9H is not good to vitiate the fortune, satvik element and causes argala to 5H of purvapunya i.e. Sanchit Karma and preventing the fruits of it to realize i.e. 9H. This concept also supports the logic of using division 9th i.e. navamsa for deciding the past birth.

Now comes the free will, wish to act of Manaha-mind i.e. Moon 4H Cancer sign dominating the free will conduct. The Sun, atma conditional soul, remembers all past incarnations and karma, but the Moon-mind is unaware of it and is free to have its own desires and outlook being forgetful and changing. Thus, qualitative disposal of Atma-Soul though static in nature seems to be constantly changing according to the free will act of mind-Moon. Soul is having restrictions of sailing within the parameter constraints of Prarabdha Karma; mind is the easy prey to constant desires flow coming thru senses i.e. Indriyas. Thus Manaha-mind over rules the soul to fulfil its desires thru Kriyamana Karma and is easy prey to the six weaknesses of senses known as weak manobal – will power. Strong Manobala and Atmabala restrict the senses and Kriyamana Karma is directed towards Tapobala ending with six strengths i.e. ShadSampata.

Vikarma [sinful or bad karma] as rising factor of curse:
Basically one's karma is the root cause of one's suffering according to the predominance of bad or worse karma and curse arises when karma is constant and extreme at worst degree.

The curse would affect according the predominance degree of the wrong doing and as per the strength of atmabala, karmabala and tapobala of the soul and native. Sage Shri Duravasa cursed goddess Laxmi to fall down from the heaven is the curse of tapobala so powerful that goddess Laxmi, the paramatmaamsa obeys it. King Shri Dasharatha with his manobala unknowingly kills by shooting arrow at invisible Shravana just by hearing sound [shabadavedhi bana] of watering pot. Shravan dead and his blind parents cursed the king Dasharatha is the example of curse of atmabala and king Dasharatha consumed the curse by his death because of separation of Lord Shri Rama his dearest son. The best example of manobala act converted to innocent or negligent 'vikarma' of Dasharatha turned to atmabala curse of separation of the son lord Rama resulting in the death of Dasharatha.

The best thing is to do our Karma the way in which it has to be done i.e. proper karma. Here our Vedas and Upanishads render us a very good guideline. 'Ishavashya Upanishad' is the best here in Shukla Yajurveda Madhyandiniya Shakha, the Veda known as Veda of Karma. The activities of the native should never be mutually in opposite to each other. Many times what we do is practically perceptible or is for material gratification but is not socially and religiously accepted. When we do the Karma only for our existence to reach the supreme soul is known as 'AKARMA'. Another meaning of this 'akarma' is desire less or unselfish karma. In the above branch of Veda in Ch-40 Mantra 2 it is said 'कुर्वन्नेवेह कर्म्माणि....kurvanneveha karmmāṇi' it is preached to do karma that is in the sole hands of the native. And in the same chapter same mantra of this branch it is said that this kind of 'akarma' will never be attached to the native and cannot be carried forward the phrase used is 'कर्म्म न लिप्यते नरे.....karmma na lipyate nare'. The duty carried for the benefits of the society and humans is defined as 'Karma'. And deeds of the native that hurts, injures, kills or makes suffering society and humans are defined as 'Vikarma'. The deeds that we should not do and which are opposite to 'Karma-Akarma' are known as 'Vikarma. 'Akarma' and 'Karma' should be done in prior harmony and we should not do 'Vikarma' is the main preaching of 'Ishavashya'. If we do this we can overcome all the weaknesses inherent inside and we can enhance our inner 'sampat'. All these Karma-Akrama-Vikarma and Shad-Ripu [weakness] & Shad Sampat [strength] are so closely knitted that we needed some micro vision for it and that is available only in our Vedas, Upnishad and Brahman Grantha.

Therefore, Vikarma is the root cause of the curse we can say.
Vedas helps us improve our karma especially Shukla Yajur Madhyandini Branch the Veda of Karma. I am giving hereunder the literature soul-knowledge of one mantra by which we can convert our Karma to proper karma and constant practice of it will put us on the path of Vikarma. This is only one mantra and just visualizes what is stored there in Vedas for us, it's time to see in our self and enhance our self-soul knowledge for the best results in our life for the sense of material gratification and in relaxation spiritual awareness, ultimate bliss.

व्वाचन्तेशुन्धामिप्प्राणन्तेशुन्धामिचक्षुस्तेशुन्धामिश्श्रोत्रन्तेशुन्धामिनाभिन्तेशुन्धामिमेड्ढ्रन्तेशुन्धामि पायुन्तेशुन्धामिचरित्रांस्तेशुन्धामि॥ मं-१४ अ-६॥
vvācanteśundhāmipprāṇanteśundhāmicakṣusteśundhāmiśrśrotranteśundhāminābhinteśundhāmimeḍḍhranteśundhāmipāyunteśundhāmicaritrāṁsteśundhāmi || maṁ-14 a-6 ||

We are not taking material object meaning [पादार्थिक अर्थ] of this Mantra. 'प्राणन्तेशुन्धामि' means to pure our breath or fresh air but its literature meaning is for purifying the soul. 'व्वाचन्तेशुन्धामि' means not to purify tounge but to purify our speech by speaking sweet, speaking truth, speaking carefully. 'चक्षुस्तेशुन्धामि' menas not to wash-purify eyes but to be vigilant and foresightedness etc. so on and so forth.

व्वाचन्तेशुन्धामि...vvācanteśundhāmi means to make pure our speech. By this phrase, Veda says whatever you speak should be pure means should have a weight. Best meaning is to enchant the Devi-Deva mantras before sleep and gain when we wake up in the morning. We always should speak truth is the way in which we can purify our speech. We should never use satire, bad, fraudulent and vulgar speech instead; we should sweetly speak truth 'सत्यं वद मधुरं वद'. The massage is 'speak sweet, speak truth and be careful when speaking'.

'प्राणन्तेशुन्धामि... pprāṇanteśundhāmi' is to make pure our soul heart. We sometimes find people very good sweet speaker but are real culprit at heart. What you speak sould be with pure heart-soul. There should be true, holy spirit in our act and behaviour. As per Vedic literature there are five winds in our body and we should purify them, then our bodily life and spiritual life can joined the process of moxa. It is said in our Upnishad 'प्राणं ब्रह्म'. What we speak should be in our heart and mind. If mind, heart and speech working in deliberate differnt way, it drag us to Vikarama is the real massage of this phrase of mantra.

'चक्षुस्तेशुन्धामि... cakṣusteśundhāmi' what you see impact on your speech and spirit is a simple experience of humankind so third phrase is to purify our eyes i.e. our sight. We should always have foresight to see in future to protect us. We should always have foresight for material happiness and thereby in relaxation spiritual awareness. Another meaning is to view & observe lord before sleep and as soon as we awake. When we see idol of our worshiped lord we should have micro vision or insight to see the virtues and potency power [aura] of god. In the modern era of television-cinema, we should not see such things, serials or episodes that knowingly unknowingly spoil our life and spirit. We always tend to lose our prudence and therefore this kind of mantras are always live to protect us, the only requisite is to have a vision and literature understanding of it. So be always vigilant to yourself and thereby to society as a whole is the massage of this phrase.

'श्श्रोत्रन्तेशुन्धामि...śrśrotranteśundhāmi' means to purify our acoustic attribute of material body so that we can hear-learn-visualize far from where we are and can make join our soul to supreme soul is the real massage. 'श्रुतं हरति पापानि' is the phrase means by listening good things our sins are removed means we find our way not to do sins and expiation for what we did. I will put this in support here means by hearing listening to Vedic literature understandings we can develop the process of real learning of spiritual and material awareness of our welfare. We can uplift our standard of living and spirit by listening to this Vedic literature is the massage of this phrase.

'नाभिन्तेशुन्धामि...nābhinteśundhāmi' this is very important and its vedic literature meaning is hard to understand but it pointed at yoga maraga [meditation]. Kundlini Yoga is advocated here I think. Powerfull and qualified guru is required for this so no comments here. The main purpose of this phrase is to protect navel from roundwarms in tropical country like Inida. The navel is mark of detached umbilicus i.e. the tube that fed us and kept us alive while we were in our mother's womb. According to Aurveda, the navel is an important site in the human body. Nearly 72,000 subtle nerves or nadis converge in this area. By the principles of Ayurveda and yoga, either the human body is made up of six chakras, with the Manipura chakra located at the spine directly behind the navel or the solar plexus, depending on the system, while its kshetram, or superficial activation point, is located directly on the navel and represents the element fire. Therefore, its purification is required for moxa marga. According to our Puranas grand lord Shri Brahma is the lord of creation incarnated from the navel of Lord Shri MahaVishnuji which pointing at the creative power of navel.

'मेड्ढ्रन्तेशुन्धामि...meḍḍhranteśundhāmi' means to purify our secret organs in broader sense. Simply we should control our Vikama. We should have a legal consensual sex with one partner to protect our physique from dreadful disease and enhance-develop our metaphysical body for ultimate bliss. It would be apt here to mention the character of Lord Shri Ramji to understand this phrase.

'पायुन्तेशुन्धामि... pāyunteśundhāmi' means to purify our feet-legs. We should go to temple every day to purify legs. The best way to purify our feet is to falling at parent's feet i.e. to take blessings of our parents & elders. We should always be ready to step forward to take on any works for developments and welfare of society. Lord Shri Ganeshaji does circumambulation of parents lord Shri Shiva-Parvati when asked to do it of earth. This is resembled to incarnation of Shri Vamana of Lord Shri MahaVishnuji where lord take away everything from King Shri Baliji for the welfare and redevelopment of the society in three steps.

'चरित्रांस्तेशुन्धामि...caritrāṁsteśundhāmi' we should always ready to purify our character thru which we establish the standard of life like lord Shri Ramji known as marayadapurshottama. When we implement the rest phrases as said above in our life I think our character will automatically be purified.

The main source of the karma is six weaknesses, which is known as 'shadripu' in Vedic literature. The source of these shadaripu is 6th house and gain of these i.e. 11th from it is 4H either sin or virtues. Again to control bad is true courage 'parakrama' is 3H or conversely loss of sins or bad virtue is 12th from 4H is 3H. Again this six weakness are not only limited to 6H but they may be scattered in duhasthana i.e. 6-8-12 houses. For instance, for Kama we sees it from 7H primarily but will turn to vikama such as forceful or non-consensual sex is seen by 8H and sex not legal or accepted by society is seen by 12H. In addition, this is applicable for all the twelve house of the zodiac. For e.g. Kama houses are 3-7-11 and forceful sex is 8H i.e. 6H to 3H, illegal or unsocial sex is 12H i.e. 6H to 7H and conjugal inability is 6H i.e. 12H to 7H and 8H to 11H. Intelligent and clever approach is required to derive the curse of any kind.

Sixth house is the source of our weakness which we refer to as our prime perpetual enemy also known as six instincts. This may be caused due to our materialistic perception i.e. 'vyavaharik buddhi' and both these are so closed knitted in our life that we cannot come out of this vicious circle. But to control and defeat these six enemies is the parakrama seen by 3H and gain-saving of this six instincts and prakarama is 4H. As per Jataka Parijata [V Subramaniy Sashtri] ch-12 verse-59 the word used while narrating the signification of 4H the word used is 'मनोगुणानि ... manoguṇāni.' To control these six weaknesses strong Moon for outer behavior and Mercury to win inner conflict and temptation is to see and also the strength and weakness of lagna lord has a lot to say in it. So we have to see 6H, 3H, 4H, 1H, Moon and Mercury to assess these weaknesses and its impact. In the run of establishing simplifying and easy method of learning Vedic astrology for name, fame and money we are doing dangerous injustice to this age old sashtra. It is never so easy to see that the native won over or defeat by his weaknesses especially in many white collared natives.

Six weaknesses [Shad-Ripu] are

[01] Kama - Desire, passions - Venus is prime factor here.

[02] Krodh - Anger - Mars & Saturn are prime significator

[03] Mada- intoxications, drugs, alcohol etc – Sign Pisces-Scorpio and the nodes are the affecting factors. Moon & Mercury is seen. Intoxication can of anything like power, wealth, self-beauty etc. etc.

[04] Lobh - Greed - Saturn

[05] Moh – Attachment –Rahu-Saturn and Venus-Moon are to see. Moha can be of anything like attachment to power and child [example is धृतराष्ट्र … dhṛtarāṣṭra] females [Indra to Ahalya], wealth, etc. etc. destroying in nature.

[06] Matsarya -Jealousy. Nodes and Saturn;

Sign signification of these weaknesses is as under.

- Aries- Anger
- Taurus- possessiveness, greed
- Gemini- desires, attachment
- Cancer - attachment, jealousy
- Leo - intoxicated by power, ego, anger

- Virgo - attachment
- Libra - kama, desires
- Scorpio - can reflect many of the Ari
- Sagittarius- anger
- Capricorn – greed
- Aquarius - dark emotions, anger, greed, possessiveness, desires
- Pisces - attachment

Counter part of these six weaknesses is six strengths [Shada-Sampat], which are as under.

1. Shama = serenity, tranquility of mind

2. Dama = self control [here by free will to get the ultimate serenity]

3. Uparati = satiety, quitism, desisting [nivartana] from sensual enjoyment or worldly actions

4. Titiksha = forbearance [xama], endurance , patience

5. Shraddha = faith [deep and firm], firm belief, purity

6. Samadhana = profound contemplation or adjustment, putting together, reconciliation.

This is in resemblance to Shri Shiva Maha Purana.
We will not go deep into to its workings and efficacy as too many exposure already done in our Vedas and Upnishads and there are many promoting school of thoughts for these and it is not our whole & sole subject

matter. Our subject matter is karma that resulted in curse and how one can come out of it in the light of astrology. There are three best ways to come out these weakness and to enhance strength are GYana maraga, Karma maraga and Bhakti marga.
By observing YAMA and NIYAMA as given in our vedic literature of shruti-smruti patanjali yoga shastra, we can control these shadripu and enhance our strength or spiritual uplifting to achieve ultimate moxa. Yama is one good observance we take to implement on our own freewill for the life time. Bhism Pitamaha has taken that yama in the form of 'bramhacharya' on his own free will for lifetime; Mahatama Gandhi observes the yama in the form of 'satya' for the lifetime. However, when we observe the restriction for a particular occasion or for the limited period, it is called niyama.

Now which blend of the above six weakness causes curse in previous adobe is very important and how we can see from the chart is our subject matter. And 'Vikarma' is the main sources and we can accordingly construe these six weaknesses like Vikama, Vikrodha, etc. which are destroying or harmful in nature to self and or others. I am explaining kama and krodha to vikama and vikrodha and rest you can judge with your prudence.

Kama- Let us take first weakness Kama and understand it how it can turn into curse, how we can protect ourselves. The rest one can understand easily. Kama is attraction between male and female, at gross material level, sex union and at transcendental level, it is pure love of soul mate. Moreover, the ultimate level is the everlasting eagerness of every jivaatma i.e. conditional soul to meet with the supreme soul parmatma. In this accord, we may divide it in three plains Kama – pure love or desire to fulfill three basic needs and the pivotal for regeneration, its devta is Kamadeva-Ratidevi i.e. Prakruti & Purusha, and its energy is Sukra's natural energy as planet this is soul mate. The Guna is Rajasik here. Vikaama – unlawful or unsocial desires or lust i.e. material level sex and desire to gather material happiness and its devata is afflicted Venus i.e. Indra for male and Mars for female i.e. Indrani or may be Indrasena. The famous episode of Indra established sex with Ahalya the Rishi patni of Gautam Rishi is the best example of this vikama and may the first of its kind for generations to come. The Guna is tamasika. Akama – No desire or no efficiency to have desires i.e. retarded or defective. Kama as a neutral element to have desire of this conditional soul to meet the ultimate supreme soul i.e. Godhead is akama. The Guna as per vedic astrology here is Saatvika. So, here also Vikama is the pivotal to curse.

Vikama – Sex by forgery is Vikama and example is Indra established sex with Ahalya the Rishipatni of Gautam Rishi and is cursed by sage Shri Gautama. In Padma Purana it is said that if the 'shudra' [lower caste by karma] do harm to the cow and or bullock [any live beings including humans]; or if the native rapes, molested, take away, or kidnap Brahman female [virgin & pious], will become impotence or nincompoop. Sanskrit verse is as under.

योनरोगोधनंकुर्यात् शूद्रःकुर्यात् विमोहितः। ब्राह्मणी हरणं वापि कर्मणा नपुंसकः॥२०॥

yonarogodhanaṁkuryāt śūdraḥkuryāt vimohitaḥ | brāhmaṇī haraṇaṁ vāpi karmaṇā napuṁsakaḥ | |20| |

Now the most important point is how we can see this in the chart that the native was ShUdra in previous birth and did this kind of vikama and or vikarma. Virgo ascendant and Pisces navamsa is to see here in the chart of the native of current birth as a starting factor. Virgo is the caste represents merchants and workers, Moha [turned into lust here] and female of Brahman caste is Pisces and other attributing factors we can confirm from the chart. This is the starting point, for which we find nexus in our Puranas and this Jyotish Shastra.

Krodha: Anger to control or harmonize or better the situation or in broader sense society-nation and humans is known as 'krodha' and is a part of our triguna prakruti i.e. Rajasik tamas. Akrodha i.e. no-anger condition means soul is in total harmony with the supreme soul to get the ultimate bliss and to give the bliss and is Sativk tamas guna. Vikrodha means anger destroying or harmful in nature to self and or others, is tamasik tamas prakruti and this can be the cause of curse.
Sage Shri DurvAsA in anger cursed 'Dharma' for taking three birth in the form of king Yudhisthir, dAsiputra Vidur and king Harischandra to reinforce the real path of religion for human race this is known as Krodha. The preaching is there in Padmapurana ch.12 of part 2. Shri Gautam Rishi cursed some deceitful rishis for their cheatings to become irreligious-unsocial, destitute of knowledge; recessional at the occasion of manifestation of Shri Gangaji River at Trayamkeshvara is the example of Vikrodha. To curse someone in vikrodha you must have acquire atmabala [strength of soul], tapobala [power of austerities] and karmabala [power of karma],

which can be the cause of sufferings to others. Shri Rishi Gautam is full of tapobala, karmabala and atmabala and the deceitful rishis became karmahina [degraded by actions] so the curse is raised. Here Vikarma vis-à-vis Vikrodha is responsible for curse and there is always vikarma nexus indicated by planetary effects as given in our puranas myth events.

Base of this work:

Now our astrological concept of Karma and Curse is clear, beautifully supported by our Puranas. When the native severely suffered, we spontaneously say it is past life karma results. Only BPHS Khemraj Edition, Mumbai has given a clue to arrive at prenatal birth karma from navamsa. And we take this as the base for this book and modify it for prudent and trained analysis.

Natal 9H is past birth position then past birth karma is natal 6H; 1H is the present birth of native and 5H is the fortune i.e. purva punya of past birth available to native in current era. This is the basic logic used here. Here navamsa lord of most afflicted nakstra is taken as 6H being starting point. 8H is nija dosha i.e. innate or inborn defect, a piercing factor telling the story of prenatal adobe. Conversely, 9H is 4H from 6H for prenatal adobe position. This entire analogy is described in chapter-10 herein this book.

Chapter-04

Prenatal Adobe as per Vedic Astrology

Why to see cursed karma of past life - Need to see past life karma or cursed karma of past life causes sufferings in form of disease, childlessness, early widowhood etc. is envisaged in this book. Our astadas smruti [18-reminiscence i.e. Hindu Law Book] clearly says that native without expiation born with some innate disease or defect or sufferings [naraka] or marks in the body.

प्रायश्चित्तविहीनानां महापातकिनां नृणाम्। नर्कान्ते भवेज्जन्म चिन्हाङ्कितशरीरिणाम्॥

प्रतिजन्म भवेत्तेषां चिन्हं तत्पापसूचितम्। प्रायश्चिते कृते याति पश्चात्तापवतां पुनः॥

महापातकजं चिन्हं सप्तजन्मनि जायते। उपपापोद्भवं पञ्च त्रीणि पापसमुद्भवम्॥

दुष्कर्मजा नृणां रोगा यान्ति चीपक्रमैः शमम्। जपैः सुरार्चनैर्होमैर्दानैस्तेषां शमो भवेत्॥

पूर्वजन्मकृतं पापं नरकस्य परिक्षये। बाधते व्याधिरुपेण तस्य जप्यादिभिः शमः॥

prāyaścittavihīnānāṁ mahāpātakināṁ nṛṇām | narkānte bhavejjanma cinhāṅkitaśarīriṇām | |
pratijanma bhavetteṣāṁ cinhaṁ tatpāpasūcitam | prāyaścite kṛte yāti paścāttāpavatāṁ punaḥ | |
mahāpātakajaṁ cinhaṁ saptajanmani jāyate | upapāpodbhavaṁ pañca trīṇi pāpasamudbhavam | |
duṣkarmajā nṛṇāṁ rogā yānti cīpakramaiḥ śamam | japaiḥ surārcanairhomairdānaisteṣāṁ śamo bhavet | |
pūrvajanmakṛtaṁ pāpaṁ narakasya parikṣaye | bādhate vyādhirupeṇa tasya japyādibhiḥ śamaḥ | |

In nutshell, humans are suffered in different forms according to their cursed karma or sinful deeds of past life according to the predominance degree of that karma. This past life karma is called cursed karma here and is to be seen as per the Vedic Astrology acumen is the basic object of this book. Expiation is also depicted here for sin free life. It is said in our astrological classics like BPHS, Bruhat Jataka, Jataka Parijata etc. that the prime aim of Vedic astrology is to see the karma of the native as depicted in the form of configuration in birth chart.

We will consider verses that relates to prenatal birth. JatakaParijata [Delhi edition of V SubramanyaShastri] in Ch.-5A verse 14-15 the adobe place of prenatal is enumerated in the following verses.

गुरुरुडुपतिशुक्रौसूर्यभौमौयमज्ञौविबुधपितृतिरश्चोनारकीयांश्चकुर्युः।

दिनकरशशिर्वार्याधिष्टतत्र्यंशनाथाःप्रवरसमनिकृष्टास्तुङ्गह्रासादनूके॥ १४॥

gururuḍupatiśukrau sūryabhaumau yamajñau vibudhapitṛtiraśrco nārakīyāṁśrca kuryuḥ | dinakaraśaśirvāryādhiṣṭatatryaṁśanāthāḥ pravarasamanikṛṣṭāsturgahrāsādanūke | |14| |

Translation - if the lord of the dreskkana [division third-D3] occupied by the strongest of the luminaries be Jupiter, the soul came out from the world of immortals i.e. Devalokain common parlance. If the Moon or Venus were the lord of the dreskkana in question, the soul-deceased came from the world of manas [humans], may be pitruloka also. If the Sun or Mars were the lord of the particular dreskkana the deceased in the previous birth belonged to the world of mortals i.e. world of deaths means 'tiryagaloka' insects, animals, birds etc. If the Saturn or Mercury is the ruler of the dreskkana in question, the departed person came from the infernal region i.e. narakaloka or inferior loka also means pretaloka, bhutaloka etc. In the previous birth, the rank of the departed was high, mediocre or low according to the ruler of the dreskkana under consideration was in the exaltation point, had fallen off therefrom or in the depression point.

Here there are two things to be clearly understood, first the verse is applicable for natives and the word used as the departed soul is for the live native as it is given under chapter 'Exit from the World'. Another one is the word used in the verse is 'udupati' also means constellation lord of Moon, but in the later part dreskkana word is used to overrule this and interpretation made by the author prevails here. I would prefer to consider benefic aspects, dignity of planet and position of depositor in application of the above verses to practical charts.

In the verse 15 of the same chapter, it is stated where the departed soul will go and from that we could infer that the 6th and 8^{th}bhava indicate past birth.

Similar proposition is made in Brihat Jataka [MotilalBanarasidas edition, translated by B S Rao] in Ch.-25 verse-14 where, the equal proposition is made. The proposition made for loka depicted there is interpreted and represented here.

Deva loka represents a higher world where superior men are supposed to go after death. Here Devas or exalted order of being is alleged to live enjoying greater privileges and higher opportunity than men do.

Pitru loka indicates that order of existence, which is inferior to Devaloka where the spirits of the dead are supposed to live.

Tiryag loka represents an inferior order of existence where men, in the course if evil careers out-balancing their good actions, are supposed to live.
Naraka loka indicates that order of existence where men with evil deeds far in excess of their good actions have to take their turns of cosmic evolution. To me narka is nothing but poor and suffering life where fruit of evil deeds are to be consumed.

BPHS by R Santhanam, Delhi Edition says in Ch. 44, Verse 41 & 42 as under.
[01] Luminaries occupies D3 of Jupiter denotes decent from the world of God
[02] if the said D3 be of Venus or the Moon the decent is from the world of Manas
[03] If be of Sun or Mars it is from the world of dead [yama]
[04] If be of Mercury or Saturn it is from hell.
This is the only prenatal adobe stage and from here, we can derive from where the conditional soul came. Important point here raised is many times it is possible that due to bad karmas of the soul, it might have taken two three birth in other yoni which is indicated as hell or tiryagyoni here and prior to those birth purva punya that of the soul earned the birth of humans. Purva [sanchit-accumulated] punya is resembled to 5H, current birth [kriyamana life] is 1H and dharma-punya [prarabdh] is 9H,automatically stands for previous birth due to which purva punya accumulated and stored for future birth, and dreskkana is the division of this three trikona is quite logical and legitimate. So, here it is construed that from 9H also we can see the previous birth position. Natural causative of this purva punya and dharma-

karma of soul is Sun and Jupiter i.e. causative of soul [1H], punya [5/9 H], dharma-punya karma [9H], child [5H] and father [9H].

According to Sachitra Jyotish of Shri B L Tahkur part-3 falit khanda-3, from 9H/L status-position of last birth can be known.

Status of the last birth:

From 9HL last birth status may be known.

From this lord planet caste [jaati], country [desha], locality [sthana] and directions [disha] of last birth can be analyzed.

If the planet is exalted, the native comes from devaloka

If debilitated or in enemy sign, comes from foreign [pasu, partum naraka etc. loka]

If own sign, friend's sign or neutral sign, comes from India [Bharat Varsa] i.e. Manushyaloka.

Last births locality as per house lord [9HL] is as under.

Jupiter = Aryavarta old undivided India

Venus-Moon = land near pious rivers

Mercury = holy and pure lands

Saturn = Blamey land which is under others domain or ruling like Muslims, Foreigners etc.

Sun = hilly and jungle land

Mars = Bihar land [geographical]

We can also consider the depositor of 9HL.

Position in last birth:

As said last birth, details can be verified from 9HL.

If 9HL is in immovable sign in D1 and D9 and it is prusthodaya adhomukha rasi then last birth was in lata-vruksha yoni. Means very neglecting, unimportant assisting [paropkari] like life.

If 9HL is in sirshodaya urdhwamukha rasi and is in moveable sign in D1 and D9 then last birth was in

pashu yoni. Means routine life, is without much expression, sense and prudence.
If 9HL is in the exalted or own sign of ascendant lord [in D1 & D3/D9] then the previous birth was in manushya yoni; if it is neutral sign of 1HL then pasu yoni and if it is debilitated or inimical sign of ascendant lord then paxi yoni. If 9HL in [D1 & D9/D3] same sign of 9HL or 1HL then last birth was in the same yoni of manushya loka. I also will prefer to take sign depositor of 9HL especially happened to be luminaries. D3 is preferred here as it indicates the form of the descent of previous birth.
If 9HL in strength then in own caste, the last birth has taken place.
According to the attributes of planets, the last birth attributes of native can be identified according the previously mentioned position of 9HL.

We will try to evaluate the chart in this respect so that we can understand how this analogy is applicable with astrological factors not mentioned but are implied and we have to use our prudence.

Ch.-1 Plvibhansli [divorced-separated within 15 days]

Date: October 30, 1986; Time: 17:15:00; Time Zone: 5:30:00 (East of GMT); Place: 72 E 52' 00", 19 N 03' 00" Dharavi, India; Nakshatra: Uttara Phalguni (Su) (24.54% left); Ayanamsa: 23-39-27.08

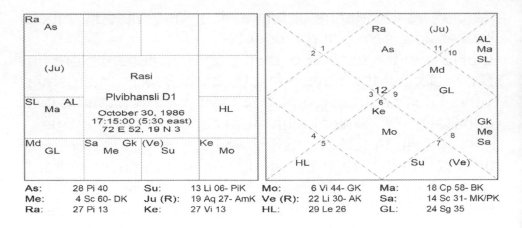

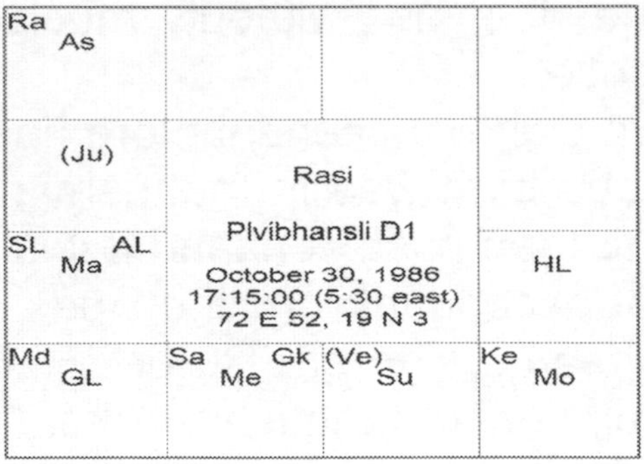

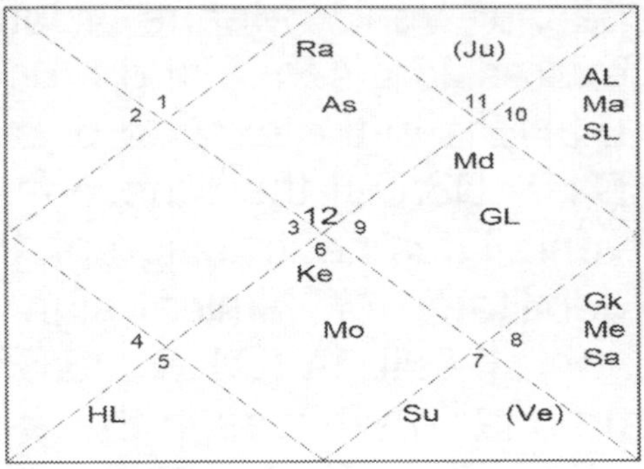

As:	28 Pi 40	Su:	13 Li 06- PiK	Mo:	6 Vi 44- GK	Ma:	18 Cp 58- BK
Me:	4 Sc 60- DK	Ju (R):	19 Aq 27- AmK	Ve (R):	22 Li 30- AK	Sa:	14 Sc 31- MK/PK
Ra:	27 Pi 13	Ke:	27 Vi 13	HL:	29 Le 26	GL:	24 Sg 35

From D3

The lady is from NarakaLoka and there her condition is bad. Sun is powerful and its D3 is taken here where Saturn is D3 lord of Sun in inimical sign having aspect of Jupiter in D1 & D3.

From 9HL

9HL Mars is exalted comes from Devaloka but having exchange with Saturn and if construed to be own sign she is from Manushyaloka and was in Blamy land and her condition was bad. 9HL Mars is in debilitated sign of ascendant lord in D1 and inimical sign of D3 the yoni is like paxi means helpless and fearful.

Ch.-2 Female [shivnigm]

Date: September 19, 1985; Time: 9:20:00am; Time Zone: 5:30:00 (East of GMT); Place: 77 E 13' 00", 28 N 40' 00"; Delhi, India; Nakshatra: Visakha (Ju) (8.05% left); Ayanamsa: 23-38-31.18

Unmarried at the age of 29th; since last 2 years skin disease is there and now is diagnosed as LP [Lichen

Planus] angular type. Lecturer at private grants college and guest lecturer in university and is double post graduate want to pursue PhD but could not succeed till the date.

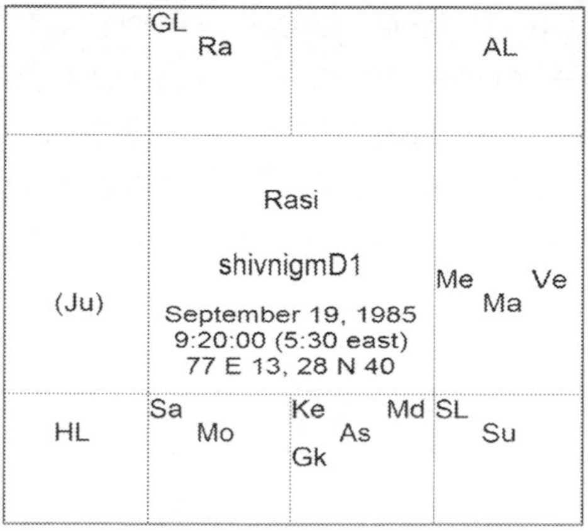

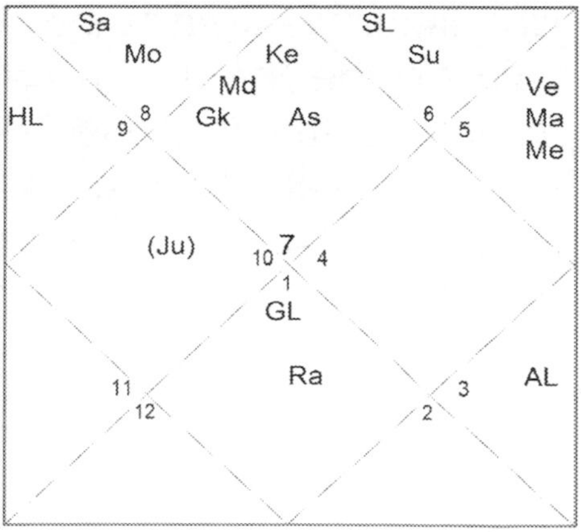

As:	13 Li 37	Su:	2 Vi 32	Mo:	2 Sc 16	Ma:	12 Le 08- MK
Me:	29 Le 22- AK/Am	Ju (R):	13 Cp 49- BK	Ve:	2 Le 46- PiK/GK	Sa:	0 Sc 12- PK/DK
Ra:	16 Ar 21	Ke:	16 Li 21	HL:	6 Sg 35	GL:	27 Ar 51

From D3

Out of luminaries, Sun is in strength as it gets 130% shadabala having natural benefice aspect of Jupiter in both D1 and D9 and is in exchange to Mercury. Sun is at 2Virgo32 degree in Mercury dreskkana means the native comes from Narakaloka. Sun is in neutral sign and her position is mediocre in narakaloka.

From 9H

9HL Mercury is in friendly sign of Sun, the native comes from Indian land i.e. Manushyaloka and is from holy land or jungle and hilly area [depositor of Mercury Sun]

9HL Mercury is in moveable sign of Leo D1 shirshodaya urdhvamukha and Aries D9 prusthodaya urdhvamukha

Here it is noteworthy that Mercury 9HL is in exchange to Sun and is posited in the exalted sign of its depositor in D3 where depositor Sun is in Virgo. Therefore, the native was in world of humans and was in jungle and hilly land was suffering doing few cruel deeds to maintain the life, might have consumed evil deeds of previous births, and now taken human birth in well to do family, capital city to consumes the rest. The nexus is there and the theory given in our Vedic Astrology is simply applicable.

Chapter – 05

Prenatal Karma and adobe from Navamsha

In BruhatParasharaHoraShastra of Mumbai Khemraja Shrikrishnadasha edition, chapter- 28 of part 1 under the head 'पूर्वजन्मवर्णनाध्यायः... pūrvajanmavarṇanādhyāyaḥ' following concept is given to understand the status quo position of previous birth era.

अथवक्ष्येविशेषेणपूर्वपापस्यनिष्चयम्। नवाम्शान्मेषमारभ्यमेषदौहिक्रमाद्वदेत्॥
1। । निशाकरनवांशधिपापंनिश्चित्यसर्वशः॥०२॥ मेषेमेषनवांशकेषुचक्रमान्मेषस्यभूयाद्वधउ
क्ष्ण्येवमपराधकंचसुधियोनिश्चित्यगोसंज्ञकम्॥ द्वंद्वेचाशवधस्तथासुनियतंगर्भेणवदेत्कर्कैसर्पव
धस्तथासुनियतंसिंहेचस्तुष्पादवधः॥०३॥ वन्यानांमृगजातीनांवधोदावानलेनहि॥ सिंहेनिश्चि
त्यमतिमान्वदेच्चांशोपरिद्विज॥०४॥ कन्यायांचवदेद्विद्वान्पापंस्त्रित्यगजंमुने॥ धनस्याहरणंव्या
जात्तुलायांचवदेद्बुधः॥०५॥ वृश्चिकेग्रामचटकेवधंचैवांडजस्यहि॥ मित्रद्रोहकृतेब्रूयाद्धन्विन्यथ
विशंकितः॥०६॥ फ़लानांवृक्षजातीनांमकरेचौर्यभेदनं। कुम्भेचैवानुसूयंतंवाच्यंविप्रविपश्चितः
॥०७॥ ब्रूयाद्विप्रधनंमीनेपूर्वार्धेतुविपश्चितः। उत्तरार्धेधनादानंतद्वधंपरिकल्पितम्॥०८॥ एकां
शेचैकजन्मस्याद्वन्द्वअंशेचैवद्विजन्मनी। त्रयंशेचैवत्रिजन्मस्यात्शेषेजन्मचतुष्टयम्॥०९॥ एवंस
र्वत्रनिश्चित्यलग्नेचैवेहजन्मनि। क्रकाद्याविप्रजन्माद्यंवदेत्सर्वत्रनिश्चयम्॥१०॥ अन्यथाजार
जोभूयात्लग्नेन्दुंनेक्षतेगुरुः। एवंचाष्टोतरशतंनवांशाःपरिकीर्त्तिताः॥११॥ क्षत्रियेक्षत्रियादीनांवै
श्येचैवविडादिकान्। शूद्रेशूद्रादिकान्वाच्यंविप्रेवैब्राह्मणादिकान्॥१२॥ परेजन्मनिजन्मस्याद्बु
ध्याचैवैहिकम्वदेत्। तदिशेस्वोच्चत्ताम्प्राप्तेमृतेस्वर्गेगतोभवेत्॥ 13। । तदीशेनीचतांप्राप्तेनरकादा
गत्यजज्ञिवान्। समत्वेचसमान्लोकान्मित्रेतीर्थेतनुं त्यजेत॥१४॥ तदीशेवारिवेश्मस्थेमृतः
प्रेतत्व माप्नुयात् ।

तस्मादागत्यजज्ञेऽसौपापंपुण्यंभुनक्तिः ॥ १५ ॥ तदीशेपापसंयुक्तेनीचेवापिस्थितेसति। वृजिनंता मसंपूर्वंकृतंतामसनिश्चितम् ॥ १६ ॥ कुजेकेतुसमायुक्तेसमस्थेराजसंवदेत्। शुभेच्चस्थितेवाच्यंसा त्विकंवृजनंबुधैः ॥ १७ ॥ अनेनैवप्रकारेणलग्नेनिश्चित्यबुद्धिमान्। इहजन्मनिसंयोज्यंक्रूरसाम्यंस मत्वकम् ॥ १८ ॥ सर्वस्यमानवस्यापिनक्षत्रत्रयमीरितम्। जन्मनक्षत्रमेकम्तुद्वितियम्मनुजन्मच। त्रिजन्मचतृतीयम्स्याद्भ्रातुव्यम्मुनिसत्तम ॥ १९-२० ॥

pare janmanijanmasyādbudhyācaivaihikamvadet । tadiśesvoccattāmprāptemṛitesvargegatobhavet ।।1।। niśākaranavāṁśadhipāpaṁniśrcityasarvaśaḥ ।।02।। meṣemeṣanavāṁśakeṣuca kramānmeṣasyabhūyādvadhaukṣṇyevamaparādhakaṁca sudhiyoniśrcityagosaṁjñakam।।03।। vanyānāṁmṛgajātīnāṁvadhodāvānalenahi।। siṁheniśrcityamatimānvadeccāṁśoparidvija ।।04।। kanyāyāṁ ca vadedvidvānpāpaṁstrityagajaṁmune।। dhanasyāharaṇaṁvyājāttulāyāṁ ca vadedbudhaḥ ।।05।। vṛśrcikegrāmacaṭakevadhaṁcaivāṁḍajasya hi।। mitra drohakṛtebrūyāddhanvinyathaviśaṁkitaḥ ।।06।। falānāṁvṛkṣajātīnāṁmakarecauryabhedanaṁ। kumbhe caivānusūyaṁ taṁvācyaṁvipravipaśrcitaḥ।।07।। brūyādvipradhanaṁmīnepūrvārdhetuvipaśrcitaḥ। uttarārdhedhanādānaṁ tadvadhaṁparikalpitam ।। 08।। ekāṁśecaikajanmasyādvandvaaṁśecaivadvijanmanī। trayaṁśecaivatrijanmasyātśeṣejanmacatuṣṭayam ।। 09।। evaṁsarvatraniśrcityalagnecaivehajanmani। krakādyāviprajanmādyaṁvadetsarvatraniśrcayam ।। 10।। anyathājārajobhūyātlagnenduṁnekṣateguruḥ। evaṁcāṣṭotaraśataṁnavāṁśāḥparikīrttitāḥ ।। 11।। kṣatriyekṣatriyādīnāṁvaiśyecaivaviḍādikān । śūdreśūdrādikānvācyaṁviprevaiubrāhmaṇādikān ।। 12।।athavakṣyeviśeṣeṇapūrvapāpasyaniṣcayam । navāmśānmeṣārabhyameṣadau hi kramādvadet ।। 13।। tadīśenīcatāṁprāptenarakādāgatyajajñivān। samatve ca samānlokān mitre tīrthetanuṁtyajeta ।।

14 | | tadīśevāriveśmasthemṛtaḥpretatvamāpnuyāt |
tasmādāgatyajajñe'saupāpaṁpuṇyaṁbhunaktiḥ | | 15 | |
tadīśepāpasaṁyuktenīcevāpisthite sati |
vṛjinaṁtāmasaṁpūrvaṁkṛtaṁtāmasaniśrcitam | | 16 | |
kujeketusamāyuktesamastherājasaṁvadet |
śubheccasthitevācyaṁsātvikaṁvṛjanaṁbudhaiḥ | | 17 | |
anenaivaprakāreṇalagneniśrcityabuddhimān |
ihajanmanisaṁyojyaṁkrūrasāmyaṁsamatvakam | | 18 | |
sarvasyamānavasyāpinakṣatratrayamīritam |
janmanakṣatramekamtudvitiyammanujanma ca | trijanma ca
tṛtīyamsyādbhrātuvyammunisattama | | 19-20 | |

Translation

Now, in special form, tells you how sins conducted in last birth era are determined. This is to be deliberated as told previously from division nine, begins from Aries and counting onwards in stipulated order. From ninth division [navamsa] of birth ascendant, Moon ascendant or from the ninth division lord of Moon position sign in birth chart be considered in assessing the status of last birth [D9 of ascendant], current birth [D9 of Moon] and next birth [D9 lord of Moon in birth ascendant]. In Aries ascendant Aries navamsa the native had slaughtered goat-ram. In Taurus navamsa [Aries ascendant] killed ox-bull-buffalo-cow etc. [or such other animal as per the eco geographical positions like nila cow, camel in desert etc.]. In Gemini navamsa is embryo slaying or deliberate abortion [bhrunahatya], in Cancer navamsa snake-serpent killing, in Leo navamsa slaughter of quadruplicates or killing it in fire to the jungle. In Virgo navamsa deserting a married woman [this is to be taken in broader sense and it includes husband or a responsible person taking care of her in absence of her husband say father or in laws etc. but in modern age the scene is changed and ladies are independent and may be construed accordingly]. In Libra navamsa it is stealing wealth by cheating, in Scorpio destroyer of eggs of birds, in Sagittarius navamsa offended friend, in Capricorn navamsa by theft plucking-cutting fruits and trees. In Aquarius navamsa offending and rebelling others and in Pisces first half vipradhanachori means taking away or cut off wealth and sacred knowledge from Brahmin by force or cheat and in second half by beating or killing him. [This is from Aries ascendant, the sage does not state what is about other signs, and we have to conclude as per our prudence and intelligence]. In first navamsa the native incurred paapa karma in last birth only, in second navamsa in two births and in third navamsa three previous birth and in fourth and onwards navamsa the naitve incurred sins in four births; in this manner from navamsa sins done in previous birth may be told. From Cancer sign etc betold varna [caste] of Brahmin etc. [4-8-12 Brahmin, 1-5-9 Kshatriya, 2-6-10 Vaishya and 3-7-11 Shudra]. If Jupiter does not give aspect to Moon or Lagna [may be also lagna lord or Moon lord] then told the child as jaraja [born to mistress]. In this custom 12*9 = 108 navamsa results are told. In navamsa if there is a kshatriya sign then tell in last birth the native was born in kshatriya caste and if vaishya sign then Vaishya and if shudra sign then shudra.[1-12]

In this manner with this astrological perception, according to the intelligent and prudent thoughts, the results of previous, current and future birth can be foretold. If lord of that said navamsa sign is exalted then at the death of last birth-attained heaven [and has come to enjoy all the heavenly happiness in this birth]. If debilitated, then came from hell, if neutral then from manas world and if friendly then the soul rested in pilgrimages and comes from there. And if navmasa lord is in watery sign then departed soul was evil spirit and after consuming that came to this manas birth to pay for his sins [paapa] and holy [punya] deeds. It is certain that if navamsa lord is with malefic planet then in the last birth had consumed tamasa yoni [pashupaxi yoni i.e. bird-quadruplicate decendant] and come to this manes birth. If navamsa lord is with Mars and Ketu in neutral sign than in last birth was in equal rajas [comfort] descendant to this manas birth. If in subha sign in exaltation then in satvik yoni and in similar way foretold yoni as satvik, rajsik and tamsik yoni same type of paapa like satvik, rajasik and tamsik in current birth. In this way, an intelligent person should foretell from the ascendant navamsa to decide the sativk, rajsik or tamsik deeds [of this birth as carried forward from the last birth]. Entire manas society is attributed to three nakshatras first is despatched soul, second is present janmanakshatra and third nakshatra is that of bretheren -relatives. [13-20]

Comments

The important note given by the sage as under is to use our prudence for final judgment to derive the sinful deeds of the native in his last, past and future birth era; I think according to the attributes, significations of the sign and planets judgment be made .

Sins of prenatal adobes as per navamsa are determined according to the schema given. In each sign there are nine navamsa beginning from Mesha. From ascendant navamsa sign, determine the sins of previous birth, from

Moon navamsa sign sins of present birth [pending karma to be completed in current era] and from Moon's navamsa of navamsa [108thDivision of sign] or from Moon navamsa lord's sign [in navamsa] future birth sins can be known. However, BPHS or other classical texts do not envisage 108th division, so we will take second interpretation. If Aries sign is, ascendant and Aries D9 sign rising, then in previous birth the native slaughtered goats-ships, and has to pay to this karma vipaka. Let us tabulate the above analogy for better perception as under. This is just like the tip of an iceberg, many things are beneath the water and we will try to understand beneath systematically in this book with practical charts.

Ascendant	Ascendant D9	Past life Karma
Aries, Leo, Sagittarius	Aries	slaughter of goats and ships,
	Taurus	kill bullock or cow
	Gemini	deliberate abortion
	Cancer	snake killing
	Leo	kill quadruplicate or kill animals by putting fire in jungle
	Virgo	give up or deserting married woman
	Libra	looting money-wealth of spammers and cheaters
	Scorpio	destruction of eggs of birds etc
	Sagittarius	betrayal to friends
Taurus, Virgo, Capricorn	Capricorn	fruit lootings and tree cuttings
	Aquarius	deceits and deceives with others
	Pisces	in first part lootings of wealth-money of Brahmin or grab it by force or forgery; in second part to take wealth-money of Brahmin by killing or beatings
	Aries	slaughter of goats and ships,
	Taurus	kill bullock or cow
	Gemini	deliberate abortion
	Cancer	snake killing

	Leo	kill quadruplicate or kill animals by putting fire in jungle
	Virgo	give up or deserting married woman
Gemini, Libra, Aquarius	Libra	looting money-wealth of spammers and cheaters
	Scorpio	destruction of eggs of birds etc
	Sagittarius	betrayal to friends
	Capricorn	fruit lootings and tree cuttings
	Aquarius	deceits and deceives with others
	Pisces	in first part lootings of wealth-money of Brahmin or grab it by force or forgery; in second part to take wealth-money of Brahmin by killing or beatings
	Aries	slaughter of goats and ships,
	Taurus	kill bullock or cow
	Gemini	deliberate abortion
Cancer, Scorpio, Pisces	Cancer	snake killing
	Leo	kill quadruplicate or kill animals by putting fire in jungle
	Virgo	give up or deserting married woman
	Libra	looting money-wealth of spammers and cheaters
	Scorpio	destruction of eggs of birds etc
	Sagittarius	betrayal to friends
	Capricorn	fruit lootings and tree cuttings
	Aquarius	deceits and deceives with others
	Pisces	in first part lootings of wealth-money of Brahmin or grab it by force or forgery; in second part to take wealth-money of Brahmin by killing or beatings

In this manner with this astrological perception, according to the intelligent and prudent thoughts, the results of previous, current and future birth are foretold. We will try to understand as under what is further elaborated by the sage. Goat and ram is the symbol of Aries sign so it is simply indicated but it means many things such as death infliction to such animals for the reasons of disease, calamity or trouble to humankind or agriculture if D9 lord of Aries is exalted. Ram is also the symbol of warrior so destroying enemy courageously is

also one of the meanings if D9 lord of Aries is exalted. We would try to elaborate the findings as under and one can derive many things accordingly. This is to repeat we should correlate sign, planet, and house significations to arrive at prudent conclusion.
Aries Ascendant and Aries navamasa rising means lagna is within 0-3.20 degree.

- Slaughter of goats and sheep, taking excitation and hasty step-decision in life and due to that causing trouble to others, family, and his forceful-violent –obstinate nature makes him deceitful and involved in theft-robbery, fraud, slaughtering means penetrating troubles like death to others are some instances of this nakshatra when afflicted. 2.00 to 3.00 degree of nakshatra if afflicted then chances of curse karma is more prone.
- Kshatriya Caste [warrior-protecting class] birth Navamsapati [D9 sign lord - Mars] if exalted then death in courageous manner and attained heaven and now comes on earth to consume its sinful-virtuous deeds.
  [D9 lord exalted-debilitated results depends on its position in D1 also as if it is debilitated-exalted or posited in own-mooltrikona-friends etc sign then the result will be changed and results be derived accordingly]
- Navamsapati [D9 lord - Mars] if debilitated then death is in cowardice manner or feared or such similar death or run away and now comes on earth to consume its sinful deeds. If also afflicted then doing sinful karmas like murder, forgery-fraud

etc. then the death, consumes preta yoni, now comes on earth to bear its sinful deeds; these effects will be seen by disease, death of loved and or dreadful event-prolonged conditions.

- Navamsapati [D9 lord - Mars] if neutral then swallowed by apparition [Maya] or sense of material gratification or such similar death and now comes on earth to consume its sinful-holy deeds.
- Navamshapati [D9 sign lord-Mars] if friendly sign then by doing good and bad karma, doing expiation comes the death in pilgrimage land and now comes to earth to consumes its sinful-holy deeds.
- Navamsapati[D9 lord - Mars] if in watery sign then by doing sinful karmas like murder,forgery-fraud etc. then the death, consumes preta yoni and now comes on earth to bear its sinful deeds.
- D9 sign lord Mars, is with malefic then consumes tamas yoni like birds & quadruplicates and now comes on earth to bear its sinful deeds and will have resemblance of such similar shapes and nature of such tamas yoni in this manas birth.
- Navamsapati [D9 lord - Mars] is with Ketu [if other lord then with Mars-Ketu] and in neutral sign then consumes similar rajas yoni [like king or king] and now bears its sinful-holy deeds in this manas birth in Rajas Yoni

- Navamsapati [D9 lord - Mars] is in exalted in benefice sign with benefic planet [say here Mars is with Venus in Pisces sign then was in satvik yoni or such similar yoni [like sages or spiritual soul] and now bear its sinful-holy deeds in this manas birth in satvik yoni.
- JanmaNakstra [of Moon or Ascendant] is three per sign and first indicates last birth, second is current birth and third is of relatives and bretheren.

This way we can construe the entire gamut of these twenty stanzas for 108 nakshatra padas. This Aries navamsa [of aswini nakshatra] elaborates as example and with the help of significations of nakshatras-stars, sign, planets, and house, we can derive the conclusions. It is commonsense that Aries navamsa of Aswini first quarter nakshatra results could not be the same as that of Aries navamsa of Magha first quarter nakshatra and we have to go according to significations of nakshatras, signs etc. and derive the conclusion according to expertise and intelligence.

If Aswini first pada is afflicted, then we will see its navamsa sign Aries wrt Ketu nakshatra lord-Mars sign lord – Mars navamsa lord. If Saturn afflicts Aries and Mars debilitated afflicted by nodes in 5H [of either D9 or D1where affliction took place] then the native might be childless and suffering from migraine or heart disease [asvini firstpada, Aries sign & 5H effect]. Maybe he blessed with child but have to face incarceration and heart disease, numerous significations with lots of variations are there, prudent application is prerequisite. Sufferings are many but how we could determine the prenatal karma is the base of this book. This is duly elaborated in Chapter-10 hereinafter.

If Magha nakshatra first pada is afflicted, then we will see its navamsa sign Aries with Ketu-Sun-Mars. Sun or Mars debilitated and afflicted with Aries sign in 11H then the native will lose his income on family-friends, facing constant wrath of dependants, involved in financial scam or ignoble source, deprive of warm love of spouse. Moreover, may be suffering as humpbacked, genetic defect in heart [7/8th from 5/4 H Leo sign of magha nakshatra signifying heart] and or left ear defect impacting brain, Jaundice, child destruction or childlessness.

These are the rewards of sinful deeds of prenatal karmas and that is to derive is the subject matter of this work. We will take practical charts and derive conclusions of cursed karma systematically for some of 108 navamsa in this book with its remedial measures in details. We will apply multiple tools available with D9 applications.

Chapter-06

Astrological Mapping of Karma & Curse

Astrological mapping of past birth and its karma is not an easy task and it is more so as we do not have any direct or manifested evidence in support. But of course, presupposing i.e. circumstantial evidence is there as the Native is suffering and is popularly known as curse of bad karma.

What is most important is nakshatra and from there we can decide the navamsa. Navamsa indicates the last birth according to BPHS as said in ch-05. The nakshatra most afflicted in the chart indicates the curse factor in terms of bad karma in the past life. Sign lord of Navamsa of the nakshatra will decide the status quo position of last birth. From this sign lord of navamsa caste [jaati], country [desha], locality [sthana] and directions [disha] of last birth can be analyzed.

If the planet is exalted, the native comes from devaloka. To repeat, Devaloka represents a higher world where superior men are supposed to go after death. Here Devas or exalted order of being is alleged to live enjoying greater privileges and higher opportunity than men. This sect also include the humans devoted to the scientific welfare and development of the society and religion; and also those who are fully devoted to GOD in its true sense and who take rebirth are called yogabhrastaatma i.e. one fallen of standard.

If debilitated or in enemy sign, comes from foreign [pasu, pitru naraka etc. loka] Pitruloka indicates that order of existence which is inferior to Devaloka where the spirits of the dead are supposed to live. Tiryagloka [pasu-paxi] represents an inferior order of existence where men, in the course if evil carries out-balancing their good actions, are supposed to live. Narakaloka indicates that order of existence where men with evil deeds far in excess of their good actions have to take their turns of cosmic evolution. Narka is nothing but poor and suffering life where fruit of evil deeds are to be consumed.

If own sign, friend's sign or neutral sign, comes from India [Bharat Varsa] i.e. Manushyaloka.

Last births locality as per house lord [sign lord of nakshatra navamsa] is as under.

Jupiter = Aryavarta old undivided India
Venus-Moon = land near pious rivers
Mercury = holy and pure lands
Saturn = Blamey land which is under others domain or ruling like Muslims, Foreigners etc.
Sun = hilly and jungle land
Mars = Bihar land [geographical]

We can also consider the depositor of 9HL.

Position in last birth:
As said last birth details can be verified from navamsa sign lord.
If navamsa sign lord is in immovable sign in D1 and D9 and it is also prusthodaya adhomukha rasi then last birth was in lata-vruksha yoni. Means very neglecting, unimportant assisting [paropkari] like life.

If navamsa sign lord is in sirshodaya urdhwamukha rasi and is in moveable sign in D1 and D9 then last birth was in pashu yoni. Means routine life, is without much expression, sense and prudence.
If navamsa sign lord is in dual sign then pitru yoni or such other degraded yoni.
If navamsa sign lord is in the exalted or own sign of ascendant lord [in D1 - D9] then the previous birth was in manushya yoni; if it is neutral sign of 1HL then pasu yoni and if it is debilitated or inimical sign of ascendant lord then paxi yoni. If navamsa sign lord in [D1 - D9] same sign of 9HL or 1HL then last birth was in the same yoni of manushyaloka. I will also prefer to take sign depositor of navamsa sign lord especially if happens to be luminaries. D3 may be preferred here as it indicates the form of the decent of previous birth.
If navamsa sign lord in strength then in own caste the last birth has taken place.
According to the attributes of planets, the last birth attributes of native can be identified according to the afore said position of navamsa sign lord. The most impactful planet will play the main role to say the bad karma converted into Curse.
We should integrate multiple tools of predictive astrology as said in our classics to arrive at prudent conclusion. At this initial stage we should look at

[01] the most afflicted nakshatra will determine the past karma turned to sufferings i.e. curse. Its navamsa sign& lord will tell us the position of last birth. This will help us find degree wise affliction of particular sign-bhava – nakshatra lord-navamsa position, simultaneously indicating the sufferings of particular influence, which

will dominate over good yoga in the chart. We have to map this with the help of multiple predictive tools available.

[02] Orbs of the planets will play its role in determining affliction of nakshatra. In General 4.30.00 to 5.00.00 degree is taken here for all planets.

[03] the most impacting planet / s has says in past birth karma. Nakshatra navamsa position will determine the same and if afflicted heavily in D9 and or D1 then predominance of evil effects will prevail. Many times we find that nakshatra lord - sign lord of nakshatra with similar significations when afflicted also indicates the prenatal karma of the native and becomes more relevant.

[04] The significations of sign, planets, nakshatras and houses are to be correlated with respect to affliction while determining the karma & curse.

[05] For the simplicity and accuracy, we will take into consideration Sudarshan Chakra method, VimsottariDasa [VSD] and KalchakraDasa [KCD], Charaparya Dasa.

We will take the chart-1 as given hereinbefore to construe this analogy.

Ch.-1 Plvibhansli [divorced-separated within 15 days]
Date: October 30, 1986;Time:17:15:00;Time Zone: 5:30:00 (East of GMT);Place: 72 E 52' 00", 19 N 03' 00" Dharavi, India; Nakshatra: Uttara Phalguni (Su) (24.54% left);Ayanamsa: 23-39-27.08

```
Navamsa                              D-9
+-------------------------------------------+
|\    Md            / \                  /|

| \     VeR     /      \              / |
|   \         /          \          /   |
|     \    /     Mo        \      /     |
|       \ /                 \  /       |
|        x Ra As AL       x Gk Su |
|       / \                / \        |
|     /     \     JuR     /     \     |
|   /         \         /         \   |
| /             \  12 /             \ |
|/                \ /                \|
|      Ma          x         HL        |
|\                / \                /|
| \              /     \            / |
|   \          /          \        /   |
|     \      /              \    /     |
|       \  /                 \ /       |
|        x     Ke          x GL        |
|       / \                / \   Sa |
|     /     \            /     \      |
|   /         \        /         \    |
| /     Me     \     /             \  |
|/               \ /                 \|
+--------------------------------------+
```

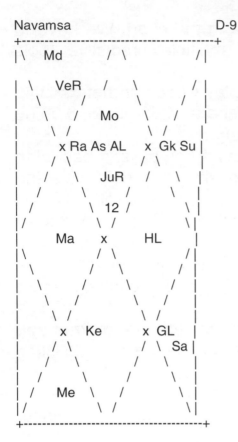

Here in D1 [given in ch-4] the most afflicted nakshatra is Sravana 2 pada at 14 degree & 5th navamsa of Capricorn that is Taurus sign, whose lord Moon is also heavily afflicted, but Mars exalted with Mars-Saturn in exchange may give some relaxation. Similarly PurvaFalguni 1 pada is afflicted by Saturn-Mars at 14 degree in Leo navamsa i.e. Leo sign and its lord Sun debilitated in D1 and inimical in D9 with heavy affliction by Saturn, Mars, Gulika and Ketu there without benefice aspect. Therefore, Sun is the indicator of status quo position in last birth. The native is from pasu-paxi loka i.e. Inferior order of existence in previous adobe and D9 sign depositor of Sun is Saturn indicates balmy land of prenatal karmas. The nexus of houses are 6th / 8th the house [12-2 H from 7H] of divorce& deceiving – wealth of spouse in D1 and in D9 11th the house of parivar and true-warm love – liquidity source [gold in those days] of spouse. The native might have deceived spouse in prenatal adobe very badly and might be involved in robbing wealth of spouse this turned in to curse and in current birth of manas she was in love with a person, married him and divorced in fifteen days only. Sun is Karaka of father and Capricorn and Libra sign represent father being 10th and 10th from 10th house of natural zodiac, father of the native left them on their own, ran away with another woman, and deserted this native and her family.

Chapter-07

Curses Yoga

Karaka or sign lord or nakshatra lord or navamsa lord defines curse or sign being impacted by at least two malefics by conjunction or planetary aspect is one view. However, I envisaged one more afflicting element over and above this like combustion, MrityuBhaga degree, Gandanta or RasiSandhi, Chhidra element, eclipses, papakartari and such other is required to raise curse or cursed karma. It is very important part of chart to prognosticate after looking at various yogas like Vaidhavya [widowhood], Janamarista [premature death], Mahavrana [dreadful disease], Klibayoga [impotent], Bandhana yoga [imprisonment], Daridrya yoga [penury] etc. We always try to remedy the yoga which gives the worst experience. As we envisage here in CH-05 & 06 most afflicted nakshatra will cause the curse and its nakshatra lord, sign lord and navmasa lord will play important role in cursed karma. If the curse is present in third, sixth, ninth or eleventh from Arudhapada the native by own action can increase the effect of curse and the suggestion is to stay away from anger, fighting, excessive intoxications, gambling, and any other form of doing harm to others. For example, if curse is in eleventh house then native is lured by good opportunity and after feeding that direction with energy the curse starts. Jupiter afflicted causes the curse of sage, Brahmin, priests or scholar, and similarly Mercury etc. planet will cause various kinds of curses as elaborated in chapter-01 as per BPHS.

Sometimes we see that Pancha Mahapurush Yoga, Raja yoga, Nabhasa Yoga etc are afflicted and the auspicious yoga is polluted or vitiated, then it could be prudently conclude that the yoga is cursed in past life and the prolonged sufferings caused. We would see this analogy in sample chart analysis where dim fit.

First we should pay attention to curses in most afflicted constellation because it shows bad intention in past life and association with respective trigunasas per attributes of nakshatra or impacting planet [tamas-rajas-satvaguna] and when benefic is strong or aspecting and planet is inYuva, Jagrat, Swastha etc. Avastha then it shows full consciousness (awakening state or scheme) is available. The strength of curse depends also on state of malefic; if the aspecting malefic is vakri remedies will not work and native must experience whole periods of concerned dasa in challenges similar to those provoked by the native in the past life(s). Shadbala also indicates the intensity of curse and if papa-kartari is present on the hosue-nakshatra-planet of the curse then it is very serious-acute one. On the other side if strong benefic like Jupiter or functional benefic aspects the curse then the remedy will be available and proficient-workable. Involvement of Atmakaraka or karakamsa or Arudha and eighth house or arudha of 8H confirms innate or inborn defect (nija dosha i.e. karmik baggage) from the past life (8th house i.e. 12th to 9H). The final confirmation comes from Shastyamsa or such higher divisons like khavedamsa [D40] and axavedamsa [D45]. Ishta-kulaDevata [5H from Jupiter or ascendant] conjunction in the curse will intensify one to remember the God as the lesson in the course of curse. We can also take planetary deity or its adhi-pratayadhi deities in this course. If still in doubt which one of the curses will be most affecting we should open Shastyaamsa [60th division- D60] and judge most afflicted planets using all standard rules.

There will be only one active curse in the chart, so the proper analysis of the natal chart is envisaged here to arrive at proper remedy if available. Nakshatra or Arudha or Atmakaraka or lord concerned in the signs of the Kala Chakra Dasa will show the source of suffering during the period. Arudhapada of bhava also plays important role in curse as for instance Shadapada (A6 – arudha of 6H) involved threatens with legal cases etc. so on and so forth. The degree period of the afflicted sign- nakshatra lord etc causing curse will be the worst and opposite for the benefic. Order is as follows: First we should pay attention to dusthana [6-8-12 house] curses from respective house, then for most afflicted one and then for the most benefics being cursed. First & Fifth being natural benefice lord is always the most benefic planet in the chart and it will always sooth and indicates the availability of doors open for ultimate bliss and the blessings available for remedial efficacy.

Sometimes the curse can come from current life and that will be visible in the praśna or transit or varsha chart as said earlier. If the ninth lord is involved the curse comes from past life is also justified in earlier chapter. Personal suffering is there if ascendant lord or Atmakaraka or karkamsa lord is involved. Eight lord relations show chronic ailments as the results, whilst tenth house involves financial issues (Arthatrikona or

Kubera House) and questionable or humiliation if malevolence impact.

Areas afflicted will be shown by most afflicting malefic-nakshatra. Here we should pay attention to natural malevolence and also the yoga. If malefic is lording two signs then the one with planet will be the source of greater challenge/suffering. We use also natural zodiac to provide information about effect of cursed karma and based on that we know that Shukra curse gives problems with finances and relationships, whilst Guru-śraapa is bad for mentor, father, studies and spending money (Pisces - twelfth house). Cursed Sun is also known as Pitrudosha and affects progeny. Jupiter curse makes one wander as the wisdom is failing (similar to weak Ascendant lord in seventh house – Brhat Parasara Hora Śastra). Mercury curse blocks one commercial prosperity and learning. Ascendant lord being cursed makes one prone to commit mistakes and Scorpio sign makes one prone to Suicide and forceful sex if female. Arudhas yuti with Ketu [damage-spoiling] will show area suffering from those mistakes.

House lorded by cursed planet suffers a lot due to the effect of that curse. If it is ascendant, then for no apparent reason one is attacked and can suffer from bad reputation, second house can destroy family and makes food polluted, 6th house can lead to loss of spouse, legal wrangles and indebtedness etc. Curses present in movable signs are more active abroad, opposite to fixed signs. The cursed planet should be analyzed in divisional charts to give auspicious advice for different areas of life. Curses which involve Upapada and 2nd lord from it will affect private life and serious relationships. Position of Venus from afflicting planet/s will show the type of challenges waiting to experience.

Timing of curse can be done by using Kala Chakra, Chara Dasa or Vimshottari Dasa. For vimshottari dasa, we look at the exact planets involved in curse (cursers and cursed). For kala chakra and Chara dasa we will verify the sign and nakshatra lord involvement.

In chart of Pushya Nakstra [pada-3] [27-August-1962; 12.30 PM; 74e07 & 22n58 +5.30 India GMT East], Venus is in Bala & Swapna Avastha and is Deena mood, Venus the D9 lord of Pushya3 is debilitated in D1, betwixt the luminaries the malefic in D9. Venus is in 11H being badhaka and more so as it carries the energies of another badhaka Mercury and 11H is 12th from 12H and 6th from 6H afflicting as a two-way sword. Moreover, Venus with kendradhipatidosa also carries the weight of arudha of 11H. Dasa tell us the time ripened for karma results that were committed in past birth. Here seeing the Vimshottari Dasa is also important as Venus MD-Rahu AD was running at the time of mishaps [02-September-2007]. And KCD is Capricorn MD – Libra AD [05-March-2005 to 05-March-2009] and the nexus is that nakshatra lord Saturn is heavily afflicted in Capricorn and Libra is the navamsa sign of pushya-3 whose lord Venus is totally lost the battle against paralysis.

Now with all other astrological acumen, we must detect the curse yoga and its time of fructifying stepwise will be dealt with in another chapter.

Chapter-08

Navamsa as per NakshatraPada

Navamsa	NakshatraPada [Natal Sign]
Aries	Aswini1[1], Magha1[5],Mula1[9], Rohini1[2], Hast1[6],Sharavan1 [10], Punarvasu1[3], Vishakha1[7], Pbhadrapad1[11]
Taurus	Aswini2[1], Magha2[5],Mula2[9], Rohini2[2], Hast2[6], Sharavan2 [10],], Punarvasu2[3], Vishakha2[7], Pbhadrapad2[11]
Gemini	Aswini3[1], Magha3[5],Mula3[9], Rohini3[2], Hast3[6], Sharavan3 [10],], Punarvasu3[3], Vishakha3[7], Pbhadrapad3[11]
Cancer	Aswini4[1], Magha4[5],Mula4[9], Rohini4[2], Hast4[6], Sharavan4 [10],], Punarvasu4[4], Vishakha4[8], Pbhadrapad4[12]
Leo	Bharni1[1],Pfalguni1[5],Pshadha1[9], Mrugshirsa1[2], Chitra1[6], Dhanista1[10], Pushya1[4], Anuradha1[8], Ubhadrapada1[12]
Virgo	Bharni2[1],Pfalguni2[5],Pshadha2[9], Mrugshirsa2[2], Chitra2[6], Dhanista2[10], Pushya2[4], Anuradha2[8], Ubhadrapada2[12]
Libra	Bharni3[1],Pfalguni3[5],Pshadha3[9], Mrugshirsa3[3], Chitra3[7], Dhanista3[11], Pushya3[4], Anuradha3[8], Ubhadrapada3[12]
Scorpio	Bharni4[1],Pfalguni4[5],Pshadha4[9], Mrugshirsa4[3], Chitra4[7], Dhanista4[11], Pushya4[4], Anuradha4[8], Ubhadrapada4[12]
Sagittarius	Krutika1[1], Ufalguni1[5], Ushada1[9], Adra1[3], Swati1[7], Satabhisha1[11], Ashlesha1[4], Jyeshtha1[8], Revati1[12]
Capricorn	Krutika2[2], Ufalguni2[6], Ushada2[10], Adra2[3], Swati2[7], Satabhisha2[11], Ashlesha2[4], Jyeshtha2[8], Revati2[12]
Aquarius	Krutika3[2], Ufalguni3[6], Ushada3[10], Adra3[3], Swati3[7], Satabhisha3[11], Ashlesha3[4], Jyeshtha3[8], Revati3[12]
Pisces	Krutika4[2], Ufalguni4[6], Ushada4[10], Adra4[3], Swati4[7], Satabhisha4[11], Ashlesha4[4], Jyeshtha4[8], Revati4[12]

Aswini 1 [1] = Aswininakshatra 1 pada and natal Aries sign, Aries navamsa;Aswini 2 [1] = Aswininakshatra 2 pada and natal Aries sign, Taurus navamsa;Degree wise nakshatrapada and navamsa sign table

Natal sign	3.2 Deg/ D9 sign& star pada	6.4	10.0	13.2	16.4	20	23.2	26.4	30.0
Aries	Aries1	Taurus2	Gemini3	Cancer4	Leo5	Virgo6	Libra7	Scorpio 8	Sagittarius9
	Aswini1	Aswini 2	Aswini3	Aswini 4	Bharni 1	Bharni 2	Bharni3	Bharni 4	Krutika 1
Taurus	Capri10	Aquar 11	Piscs12	1	2	3	4	5	6
	Krutika2	Krutika3	Krutika4	Rohini 1	Rohini 2	Rohini 3	Rohini4	Mrugsirsa1	Mrugsirsa2
Gemini	7	8	9	10	11	12	1	2	3
	Mrugsirsa 3	Mrugsirsa4	Ardra1	Ardra2	Ardra3	Ardra 4	Punarvasu1	Punarvasu2	Punarvasu3
Cancer	4	5	6	7	8	9	10	11	12
	Punarvasu4	Pushya1	Pushya 2	Pushya3	Pushya4	Ashlesa1	Ashlesa2	Ashlesa3	Ashlesa4
Leo	1	2	3	4	5	6	7	8	9
	Magha1	Magha2	Magha3	Magha4	Pfalguni1	Pfalguni2	Pfalguni3	Pfalguni4	Ufalguni1
Virgo	10	11	12	1	2	3	4	5	6
	Ufalguni2	Ufalguni3	Ufalguni 4	Hasta 1	Hasta 2	Hasta 3	Hasta4	Chitra 1	Chitra2
Libra	7	8	9	10	11	12	1	2	3
	Chitra3	Chitra 4	Swati1	Swati2	Swati3	Swati 4	Visakha1	Visakha2	Visakha3
Scorpio	4	5	6	7	8	9	10	11	12
	Visakha4	Anuradha1	Anuradha2	Anuradha3	Anuradha4	Jyestha1	Jyestha2	Jyestha3	Jyestha 4
Sagittarius	1	2	3	4	5	6	7	8	9
	Mula1	Mula2	Mula3	Mula4	Pshada1	Pshada2	Pshada3	Pshada4	Ushada 1
Capricorn	10	11	12	1	2	3	4	5	6
	Ushada2	Ushada3	Ushada 4	Shravan1	Shravan2	Shravan3	Shravan4	Dhanista1	Dhanista2
Aquarius	7	8	9	10	11	12	1	2	3
	Dhanista3	Dhanista4	Satbhisa1	Satbhisa2	Satbhisa3	Satbhisa4	Pbhadra1	Pbhadra2	Pbhadra3
Pisces	4	5	6	7	8	9	10	11	12
	Pbhadra4	Ubhadra1	Ubhadra 2	Ubhadra3	Ubhadra4	Revti1	Revti2	Revti3	Revti4

D1 = natal chart i.e. division one chart

D9 = navamsa chart i.e. division nine chart

Chapter- 09

Terms used for curses

There are various types of sinful, evil, or ill act karmas giving rise to Curse that we will refer to as cursed karmas hereinafter. There are many terms used for cursed karmas and most popular is 'DOSHA'. Dosha is a defect and nobody is embodiment of perfectness, so it is inherent every where and in everyone, it is another perception that we do not know. However, among pundits and astrologer DOSHA is curse such as the term 'pitru dosha' used for 'pitru shaapa' the most popular one. Nevertheless, in reality curse does not rise in common and the native could not be able to know generally and can only be known after suffers setback or event occurred such as early widowhood, dreadful diseases at young age, early child loss etc. What astrologers are doing for pitrudosha is nothing but prêt sraadha etc. without finding the truth behind these entire gamuts of curse in the chart. The curse only rises if your ill acts resulted in death or trouble like death and its suffering is also such terrible.

Pitru Runa [Karmic Debt] - When we enjoy something which is not ours in any way, then it is a kind of obligation and is known as runa, we have to liberate the same in the current birth or the next one. Moreover, for that our kalpa sashtra provides for daily tarpana, paravana shraddha [popular as Mahalaya Sharaddha or tithi sraddha] once in every year when sun is in Virgo sign and Bhadra Masa Pitru Paxa is running and tirtha snana-sraddha, dana dharma etc. as elaborated. There is also for every yagna karma or sanskar karma [naama karana sanskar, annaprasana sanskar etc] there is a provision for nandi sraddha to take blessings and to give pitrus basic five needs. Naandi in Sanskrit means pleasing i.e. pleasing Pitrus. This is because pitrus are given status as Deva popularly known as Pitru Deva or Pitru Naarayana. When we fail to do the same, pitru runa is not removed and we indebted the karmas of our conditional souls. This is the starting point of pitru dosa.

Even one pitru tarpana and paravna shraddha in a year will liberate you form pitru rina. But we are so busy and so indulged in our karma that we do not bother to do this as if parents always stand for betterment in our favour.

In each life, we have mother, father, brothers, sisters, spouse, and children and so on. We are born in a family because of undercharged debts of past lives. Constantly we are creating accounts, debiting and crediting. We are creating Karmic debts with all those with whom we interact. The Karmic debts (Runa*)* lead to bondage or attachment (bandha*)*. This karmic attachments draws us into the circle of existence again and again with the same and different entities is at the root of repeated births is one view.

Karma concludes to some Runa, Runa again leads us to karma, and this is like two-way path. If you have given something to or taken from somebody without any consideration and is not returned back in lifetime it will be carried – stored in the soul's micro body. In the next birth, this has to be carried and will be fulfilled in the manvanubandha. If the karma involves materialness and out of natural love and affections then this manvanubandha [known as line of descendants or tie-up or union link] will be seen as parents, child, spouse, co-born, cousins etc. etc. Again, if we do karma with mal intentions and ill mind in past birth, it will come to you in next birth with bitter relationship or enmity. In most of the cases, this karmic debt ensures a complementary fit, just like lock and key over which you do not have control and is auto operative.

Pitru Dosha - What is Pitru Dosa is not easy to explain that though popular the term is. Plain meaning is harmful pitrus or defective pitrus or wicked pitrus etc. Actually, there is no defect or harm in Pitrus as they stand as Deva and their magnanimity [prashanntta] is equal for all lineal ancestors. The problem lies in us that we could not take the serenity of them by not doing our daily and yearly Karmas for pitrus or more particularly could not care to do proper sraddha vidhi for them for their mukti and to relieve ourselves from Pitru Runa. This is the first and foremost step toward Pitru Dosa.
Karma is that force which is accumulated through a person's deed i.e. sva karma in past life. One will have to encounter in this life the good and the evil influences of his karma. Past life, karma is called 'sanchit karma' being carried forward in current birth era. Other kind of karma we carried in this birth era is 'sansargik karma' i.e. bad or good influences of karma of our pitrus where we are under their obligation in terms of enjoyment of their wealth and properties bequeathed or they are the part and parcel of our livelihood-welfare etc. If karma

influence is good it is Pitru Krupa and if bad it is Pitru Dosa. Ignorance of pitru karma is not an excuse, one has to suffer-enjoy for that as if they fall under lineage.

This is the base of our Astrology to understand and realize Karma of the native and Kalpa Sastra is a way out to take the ultimate bliss of our Gods and Pitrus.

As we, all know that to maintain the livelihood-welfare of family and self, the lineage ancestors committed such deeds that may be termed as bad in our sashtras and the part, which is enjoyed as a family member, is passed over in as much as we enjoyed. This is the base of pitru dosa for bad karma of conditional soul in past.

There are three categorical conditions; one is death after sinful karma, death of akaal mrityu and death in trance or stoic etc. Sometimes our ancestors do such sinful karma that their final emancipation of soul is obstructed and the soul could not take either pitru yoni or other yoni and hanged up in between called prêt yoni and constantly in anxiety for getting moksha or mukti. And, during this process the soul urge to their lineage - ancestors by doing some trouble and obstructions. This is called Pitru Shaapa as popularly known but in Sraddha Karma it is known as Pitru Badha. Also due to akaal mrityu the soul could not take either pitru yoni or other yoni and hanged up in between called prêt yoni and constantly in anxiety of getting moksha or mukti. And, during this process the soul urge to their lineage ancestors by doing some trouble and obstructions. This also falls under Pitru Shaapa or Badha as said.

Which are bad karmas, in full details elaborated in our sastras and we have to relieve our pitrus and our self as well from that. This is called हेमाद्रि संकल्प (hemādri saṁkalpa) and after hearing the same bathing and donation dan-daxina to Brahmin is provided. This is one part of pitru dosa nivriti karma.

What is akaal mrityu or untimely or unwanted or unwarranted death [durmarana] is well elaborated in every standard shraddh karma classics. There are 36 kinds of durmarana and 64 kinds of durgati mentioned in our shastras.

Very beautiful way is given for understanding what sinful karma and akaal mrityu is and how we can relieve our Pitrus and ourselves from that. Human has no control over death and also Karma of conditional soul. So, there is no reason for fear and blind faith; only proper vision is required. Now irony is that what is stated as sinful is applicable to all either one way or the other, no body spared, it is inevitable. So it cannot be cursed and but probable sinful karma of the departed soul and the native.

Still there is Pitrus i.e. past soul who does not get ultimate mukti for whatsoever reason and they are not in pret yoni and are waiting for mukti also fall under this Pitru Shaapa. Such past souls are retarded or unconscious death etc. Those Pitrus who are in trance [mohaavstha] or stoic [udaasin] or annoy-angry or such other condition are also comes under this category and are required to be relieved through Nandi Sraddh.

Pitru Dosa or Srapa or Shaapa or Runa or Baadhaa:

Pitru Runa is an obligation we inherited by bith and is always in one way or the other will accumulate to some extent during our life tenure. This is well-elaborated hereinabove.

Pitru Shaapa is a kind of curse [Shaapa i.e. curse and not Sapa which means serpant] for which the native has to suffer. This is more or same to the Pitru Dosa as envisaged by our sastras with the difference that dosa is defect of negligence and shaapa means abuse or curse given by pitrus because of which we are bereft of things seen by our birth charts. As we have seen that the term pitru includes wide range of souls and we experience the sufferings of childlessness or something like that which called 'sapexa' in Sanskrit but could not know or visulise the reason is called 'anirdista' in Sanskrit. This is Pitru Shaapa, more severe than the Pitru Dosa as it certainly indicates the souls hanged up in Pret Yoni or such other abusing Yonis and its results are also the worst.

Pitru Dosa is a kind of defect that is raised from our negligence or the defect of karmas of the past souls, both 'sva karma' and 'sansargik karma'.

Pitru Srapa is raised due to the blemished inheritance in terms of materialness accumulated by our pitrus by unwarranted source or sinful karmas.

Pitru Badhaa is in general trouble or suffering caused by past souls. When pitrus are in pret yoni and do not get ultimate mukti, they do some trouble which is known as badha or pida in Sraddha Karma. So we shall take Pitru Shaapa included Pitru Badha.

Kuldevta Dosa, Deva Dosa, Pitru Dosa, Graha Dosa: There are too many kinds of Dosas as captioned above but that does not mean that it embodied in Devas or Grahas or Pitrus, as their magnanimity is equal for all. For instance Sun will never say that one will get this much morning rays and other will that much, but the base is that we ourselves have some defect [of sleeping] to get it which is reflected by chart and here astrology helps to see the defect and that is why astrology is called "eyes" of Veda.

Planets and Pitru Dosa or Pitru Shaapa:

We can only see pitrus shaapa in astrology through the planetary-house jugglery. Rahu-Ketu are construed to be the main karaka of pitru dosa. Rahu is karaka of pitrus in stoic, trance, annoyed condition, Saturn shows defects and Ketu is Shaapa includes pitrus in Pret Yoni or such other dreadful-harmful conditions. Rahu-Ketu also indicate serpant yoni and Saturn-Ketu shows cemetery or like conditions, Rahu-Mars chronic disease death or rebellions or blasting angry or like conditions. All this kinds of past souls troubles us . So Rahu-Ketu are main karakas of pitru dosa and when Mars-Saturn or such other functional malefic joins with house lord and karakas then dosa will be converted in acute shaapa and can be seen from various angle like 5H shaapa and can be seen from various angle like 5H childlessness, 4H motherless-parentless, 9H fortuneless [bhagyahin] and so on.

Most of the classics on the topic of santan pratibandhaka [childlessness] give the clear work of pitru shaapa. And one can equally find pitru dosa as per intelligence and prudence as said in above topic. We can also apply these combinations to the karakas planet and house for viewing pitru dosa to that respective karakas. For instance, rahu-ketu in 2H or 4H means the pitru dosa is from own house or family. Please remeber that Pitru Dosa is a defect or negligence and Pitru Shaapa is more than that and our pitrus want mukti as they are in pret yoni. You will find pitru dosa in every chart or divisonal charts as Rahu-Ketu are part and parcel of that dosa and when luminaries joins it becomes acute. But for Pitru Shaapa one more functional malefic like Saturn and Mandi or Gulika is required in my view. Please understand this and our Sage like Shrimad Yogiswar Daivagna Parashara in BPHS, has rightly used the word Pitru Shaapa; we are blessed for giving this understanding as sages do not teach us every part explicitly, but we have to understand it as per our prudent intellect for the welfare of human being.

There are various shaapaa elaborated in our classics like BPHS as per karaka tatvas of planets as under.

Sun= Pitru
Moon= Matru
Mars= Bhatru

Saturn= Pret or ghost, sinful soul, animals
Rahu= Serpant or trance, stoic etc. soul
Ketu= Serpant or troublesome soul, dog etc.

Remedial Measures:
We are not here to discuss in detail the remedial measurs for Pitru Shaapa [Popularly known as Pitru Dosa, which is not correct]. In most of the region Narayana Bali Shraddha or Panchbali Sraddha is suggested to overcome this blemish. Pancha Bali is suggested to cover up shaapa like sarpa, preta, matul shaapa, bhuta badha etc. There are other remedial measures also availble like Pitru Shanti Pooja, Mantra Japa Anusthana, Parvana or Mahalaya Shraddha or Shrimad Bhaagwat Saptaha Paraaayana etc. There are also other remedial measures mentioned in BPHS and will treat them separately. We are not here to judge, which is best or better.

The sage Shri Parashara in his treaty in first chapter is segregating and unifying the power of lord in humans and power of élan in lords and vice versa. The sage sees how lord and humans are different and by way of unifying the power of lord in humans and power of élan in lords and vice versa. This makes human being to think and feel that there is always the power of divine values built in values inherent and the native should be aware of it to make good. Divine values can be triggered up by doing all auspicious and good things as indicated in this book that is to say by way of remedial measures. Environmental values obstructing the native can be warded off vigilantly and for this also lot of remedial measures are available like "pranayama," can be warded off vigilantly and for this also lot of remedial measures are available like "pranayama," "yoga," "yagya", "jap" and so on. What are the reasons to deviate the native from begetting the soul peace or divine textures and what are the remedies to overcome this is in detail elaborated in various theories of Vedas, Upanishads, Shruti, Smrutis, Adhyatma Chintan etc. etc. etc. and is not our subject matter here. Our subject matter is power of planets, signs and related governing dictums of astrology.

According to my understanding of *jyotish* as hinted by the sage in the BPHS, these *jeeva ansha* (referred to as J hereinafter) and *parmatma ansha* (referred to as P hereinafter) are the virtues of planets co-existed in the native and at a time segregating and unifying. The only requisite urge (in the form of analysis of chart) is to identify it and to use it for all round betterment of the native for either material happiness or spiritual peace or both as well. These virtues are given in most of all the classic texts on Vedic astrology. These two elements of J & P are two different powers of planets. J is the power of planets embodied in all living beings and P is the another texture of planets available to all in its natural way in equality, only degree of predominance may differ. The embodied texture J of planets can be altered with the help of power of P to get desired results. The resultant effect is that whenever the native predominate the power of P, he becomes more spiritual and is able to give and get the ultimate bliss and whenever he predominates the J, he become materialistic and is not able to get and give ultimate bliss. J is the kind of

Mayashakti i.e. conditional texture of soul that is the *Karmavipak* i.e. repenting texture of P.

Another view is that Maha VishnuJi's Viswaroopa Darshana in which all (planets) Surya, Chandra and other grahas pour energy and get charges from the lord of lord. In Nature, we find it as a charger. It is same for all living and non-living matter. The lord of lord has both unifying and segregating powers to indicate how humans are different from Gods and make them also feel the divine powers inherent can be applied as and when needed. The words may not be enough to give a verbatim. Temperamental is environmental effect in humans etc. when we apply for correctional methods, the need for divine power is to be revoked according to the physical state of the planets as agni, prithvi, jala and akasha tatwas. And here we can seek these sources of energies in the form of grahas, their adhi devta and prati adhi devta.

Mains remedy available in shraaddha karma:

To overcome Pitru Shaapa or Baadhaa or Dosa or Rina following are the basics provided in our standard shraaddha karma with other procedures.

- Expiation of sinful karma or bad karma by हेमाद्रि संकल्प hemādri saṁkalpa) and after hearing the same bathing and donation dan-daxina to Brahmin.
- Durmarana [akaal mrityu] expiation; this includes all kinds of undisrable death and death not known.

and to give it *daampatya jivana* is also a very holy deed is included here. 'Utsarga' means 'tyaaga' i.e. liberation. Substantial meaning of this term is castration of vrishabha means bull but literal meaning shows that 'vrishabha' is the symbol of 'aatmaa' and 'gau' [cow] is 'punya karma'. And with the help of punya karma derived from shraadha-daana-bojana-dharma karama helps 'aatmaa' getting 'mukti'. Also we have to leave behind all our body's and soul's hallucinations or stoic or such condition and help in getting 'parama mukti, is also included in this 'utsarga kriya'.

- Pind Daana is for eternal contentment [axaya tripti] of souls.

Please understand this so there will be no fear and blind faith regarding our pitrus. We have no controls over the death and karmas of conditional souls.

Chapter-10

Prognostication of cursed karma

Bad Karma raised to curse called cursed karma and detected from the worst afflicted star in the chart.

We have seen in CH-06 that the navamsa sign lord of the star most afflicted in the chart indicates the status quo position of last birth. From this sign lord of navamsa caste [jaati], country [desha], locality [sthana] and directions [disha] of last birth can be analyzed. How we can map this is elaborated therein. In Ch-07 curse yoga is elaborated as curse is defined by karaka or sign lord or nakstra lord or navamsa lord or sign being impacted by at least two malefic by conjunction or planetary aspect is one view. Moreover, I envisaged one more afflicting element over and above this like combustion etc as depicted below.

Now I am presenting the overall theme to assess the cursed karma and its timing to realize the rewards i.e. suffering there to with shastrayik base of astrology. We should integrate multiple tools of predictive astrology as said in our classic to arrive at prudent conclusion of cursed karma.

[01] Most afflicted nakstra will determine the past karma turned to sufferings i.e. cursed karma in the form of disease, childlessness, wifelessness etc. The basic analogy is asunder.

(i) Most afflicted nakstra degree in D1 is the primary source of prenatal karma in the form of sufferings along with its sign, sign lord and nakstra lord.

(ii) Navamsa sign and its lord of most afflicted nakstra give the clue of prenatal karma.

(iii) 8th hose from the most afflicted nakstra degree or its D9 lord also gives the clue of prenatal karma to a living being for which the native came in the current birth era to consume the results.

We have to segregate and unify this analogy to come to prudent conclusion. This helps us understanding the sufferings of current era due to cursed karma of previous birth.

[02] Orbs of the planets will play its role in determining degree affliction of naskstra. In General, maximum +/- 4.00.00 to 5.00.00 degree orbs taken here for all planets. With your expertise and proficiency, you may narrow the gap of this orb degree.

[03] Apart from most afflicted nakstra, one more element envisaged here. Combustion, Mrityu Bhaga degree, Gandata or Rasi Sandhi, Chhidra element, eclipses, papakartari , presence of Gulika /Mandi and such other is required to raise curse or cursed karma. It is further said there that avastha [Mood, Alertness etc.] of planets, Shadabala [six strength], triguna attributes [satva-rajas-tamas] of impacting nakstra or planet, involvement of pada – arudha/upa, Karkamsa, etc are important and play their role in deriving cursed karma. The final confirmation comes from Shastyamsa [D60] or such higher divisions like khavedamsa [D40] and axavedamsa [D45].

[04] Sometimes, we find that there is more than one star quarter afflicted heavily in the chart then with the help of orbs, we should confirm the degree position in higher divisions like D60, D45 or D40. We should confirm this

taking divisional chart independently, which will give us tripod or multilateral affliction of D1, D9 and D60/D45/D40.

This is because amsa that gives you the results and not the sign and house as a whole and that is the reasoned logic behind the entire gamut of divisional chart in Vedic astrology.

[05] Karaka Element should also be either afflicted or weak

[06] Dasa system applied with transit to assess the timing of fructification of cursed karma. Kala Chakra Dasa [KCD] or Chara Dasa or Vimsottari Dasa should be applied to study this sacred lord of cursed karma. The working efficacy of this dasa system is out lined below.

- Dasa Planet-sign is afflicted in natal chart as derived in point [01] *supra*.
- Dasa of this afflicted planet-sign exists or any planet having relationship with it in natal chart as per standard dasa rules to fructify the results.

[07] Sudarshan Chakra system with its dasa [SCD – sudarshan chakra dasa] is applied to confirm the house prevailing at the time of dasa with its significations matching with the sufferings or fatal event of the chart. This may or may not be envisaged as per the expertise of the astrologer.

[08] Maha Dasa or Antar Dasa or SCD planet-sign is again afflicted in transit in the following manner.

* Hard core malefic is in the 1H to dasa planet-sign

* Hard core malefic is in 6-8-12 house to dasa planet-sign

* Hard core malefic aspect the dasa planet and or sign

Now benevolence influence this natal & dasa planet-sign indicates that expiation or remedial measures will help the native but if such impact is weak or retro in nature then remedial measures might not work in *toto*. In the same manner multilateral benevolence impact on the natal and dasa planet-sign will govern the pious and holy deed i.e. punya karma of the native and the results are auspicious.

[09] Cursed karma of past life & Expiation

In various chapters, we tried to give different options to determine the prenatal adobe place, caste etc and the basic analogy to arrive at prudent conclusion of past life karma which we will referred to as cursed karma for which the native suffering in current birth era.

General Exception-

If there is any benefice, element relation to the above analogy will rule out or keep minimal the suffering or cursed karma according to its predominance degree. This means fortunate, auspicious, or benevolent planet or element and this may includes karaka and natural or functional benefice relation to the house and lords referred here. Karakas elements are well elaborated in our various classics and we have to see there. Auspicious or fortunate elements are shubha graham in Kendra or trikona to the respective house or planet in shubha Vargas or vaishesikamsa or birth in amrit gati etc.

I have used multiple tools to determine the past life status quo position and karma and most of them are depicted here.

Chapter- 11

Attributes and Significations of Asterism, Sign, House and Planets

There are number of classics and modern literature available on Vedic astrology that in detail elaborated the attributes and signification of planets etc. and we will not discuss it here. There are numerous disease and sufferings in this manes world and one is not able to record it under one chapter. However, we will try to summaries some details to get first sight idea.

House Significations:

House	If afflicted Suffering caused in that part
1H: General health and happiness, status, body complexion, qualitative disposal; **Body parts**-; head, face, brain, facial bones, pituitary glands, cranium bones,	Paralysis, giddiness, wounds/ scars to head, erratic endocrine glands, derangement, brain fever or bleeding or disorder, stupidity, nose-bleeding, problems at birth time, every kind of suffering is to be seen with the help of this etc Karaka are Sun and Mars, Natural Zodiac sign Aries.
2H: Wealth, family, status, fortune, Body- speech/tongue, vision/ right eye, neck & bones, nose/ throat /trachea/ larynx/ tonsils, cerebellum/ cervical region & bones.	Problems to eyes, sore throat, thyroid glands, cervical, gums and teeth, speech, etc Karaka is Venus
3H: Younger brothers or sisters, courage, short journeys, writing and communicative capability; environment to interact with society; **Body parts**- shoulders/collarbones, arms / grabbing, right ear, trachea/mental equilibrium, spine & nervous systems begins etc	Problems of respiratory canal, asthma, tuberculosis, shoulder pains, fracture in the collar bone region, mental disorder, partial deafness, nervous non coordination with muscles, beginning of spinal cord, etc.; Karaka is Mercury
4H: Mother, education, vehicles, domestic peace/inner feelings, properties, mind, **Body parts-** heart & emotions. Chest/ breast and lungs	Coronary problems, lungs / chest/ breast cancer or disorders, emotional disorders, lunacy and the problems connected to the circulatory systems;

	Karaka is Moon, for intelligence academicals Mercury Vehicle Mars-Venus.
5H: Intelligence, speculative gains, conception, learning, position, inclinations, spiritual pursuits, **Body parts-** stomach/belly, gall bladder, pancreas, diaphragm, spleen, liver, spinal cord, etc.	Diabetes, peptic ulcers, anemia, weak heart, digestive power problems; colic pains, stones in gall bladder, acidity, , dyspepsia, diarrhea. Sun is karaka of spinal cord [read with 3-7-11 H], pleurisy, lack of fertility, menstrual Problems. ; karaka is Sun & Jupiter
6H: Disputes, debts, enemies, maternal uncles, employees, diseases, losses through theft and fire; **Body-** intestinal function, appendix, ovaries, fallopian tubes, lower abdomen/colon, kidney, etc in 6 diseases arise mainly through faulty indigestion or weak immunity.	Constipation, hernia, blood urea and nervous breakdown. poor digestion, mal absorption, gas, constipation, ulcers, food allergies, hypoglycemia, diabetes and appendicitis, along with immune system weakness; Karaka is Venus, tube and chambers in body karaka is Mercury and live process in this is Moon. Servant[job], Disease and suffering karaka is Saturn
7H: Wife, partnerships, conjugal life, home abroad, travel etc; **Body-** sex urge/urine. loss of memory or eyesight, pelvic girdle, vagina, uterus, cervix, lumbar region, etc.	Venereal diseases, gout pains, urination, impotency for women, sterilization, renal /urine, kidney problems, Spine nerves etc; Karaka is Venus & Moon
8H: longevity, inheritance, accidents, obstructions, losses, misfortunes, disgrace, easy gains, disappointments; **Body-** anus, hip, testes, varies, etc..and permanent diseases. The 8 indicates congenital or vitality problems, including atastrophic or debilitating diseases and epidemics.	Urinary infections, boils, hemorrhoids, rectal cancer, hydrosol, fissure, blood disorders, impotency in men, and venereal diseases Karaka is Mars and for longevity is Saturn
9H:Ffather, preceptor, spiritual learning, inclinations, past deeds, meditation. foreign travel. and education, general fortune. Pilgrimages; **Body-** thighs, thigh bones. bone marrow, hip joints and the arteries	Low productivity of blood, thallasemia, leukemia, high fevers, obesity, arteriosclerosis, paralysis below the waist, Arthritis or injury to the hips. Karaka are Sun and Jupiter

10H: Represents profession, status, karma in life, character, ambition, next birth, happiness from male progeny; **Body- knee** joints and bones, body gait/pace	Arthritis, broken knees, inflammation of joints, general weakness and emaciated body. Weak bones. Karaka is Sun, commerce Mercury and karma karaka is Saturn
11H: gains, friends, elder brothers, income, prosperity; **Body-** shanks/calves, left ear and left arm, right footprint (accomplishments) recovery from sickness	Weak lower legs, pain/cancer in legs, poor blood circulation, low productivity of blood, circulatory problems, weak nerves [Spine end], Karaka is Jupiter & Sun Saturn as natural zodiac sign
12H: expenses, losses, end of life, life in foreign lands, obstructions in life, separation from family, imprisonment, pleasures of bed; **Body-** left eye, lymphatic system, ankles and feet. Loss of limb/amputation/ crippled limb. Teeth, handicaps, suicide, chronic ailments. 12th indicates weakness, debility or hospitalization.	Problems to the body parts governed by the house and weak immunity. lymphatic disorders, hypoglycemia, diabetes, tumors, trouble with the feet and fungal infections. Karaka is Jupiter, Moon,

Seven Constituent of the Body:

Seven Dhatus (tissues)	**Karakas, & Notes**
PLASMA, - Rasa	Strong Moon provides good hydration to the body, Afflicted Mercury. can cause skin diseases, which often arise from a sensitive mind and nerves .
BLOOD - Rakta	Sun that governs the heart which drives the blood, Moon as governing bodily fluids, of which the blood is the most important, & Mars as the planet causing most Pitta and blood disorders.

	Karaka of Blood is Mars, Chandra being live process producing blood , Sun as karaka of heart purifying the blood
MUSCLE- Mamsa	Mars is a planet of work and action, & Saturn, which is responsible for the structure of the body
FAT- Meda	Meda Jupiter is the main planet responsible for bulk, Moon's role to allow us to hold water and weight
BONE- Asthi	The bone is the main Vata tissue in the body and is connected to the absorption of Prana in the large intestine, both of which relate to Saturn & Sun because only if the Sun is strong and digestion good can the bones be properly built up.
NERVE -MARROW - Majja	Mercury = nerves (gray marrow); Mars related to the red marrow. Saturn and Rahu as causing nervous system disorders, largely by depleting the nerve tissue, should not be overlooked
REPRODUCTI VE Seminal fluid	Reproductive fluid. The strength or weakness of

	the reproductive system connected to the placement of Venus in the chart. plus the Moon's general role in fertility

Signs:

Sign	Long/Short	Sign Indicators	Body Parts	Interaction with Lagna / House
Mesh	S	Energy, activity, aggressive and healthy. in case Mars is strong and beneficially disposed	Head, Face, brain, cranial and facial bones, Mind ,Physical body ,Headaches, carotids	In 1H, Body is like Mars or sun if strong, influenced by aspects or conjunction. If Mars is weak the native suffers from wounds, fevers, short-tempered, diseases of impure blood, inflammations
Vrushabha	S	Signifying materialistic pursuits and comforts, precise, temperate,, gives a healthy constitution, a strong Venus gives good health, otherwise weak nerves.	Neck, throat/tonsils, gullet, cerebellum , bones of the neck, Tongue, voice, right ear, Teeth , Eye sight, right eye	Strong Venus in 1H gives poor health and in 8 or 12 H gives sickly constitution, impact the body parts indicated
Mithun	M	Talkative, ambitious, imaginative, locomotion, communication, general relationship and interaction, intelligence, grabbing [finger]	Shoulders, upper arms and upper chest, hands and their bones , fingers lungs, throat/ breath, spine and nerves system begins,	Strong Gemini afflicted by mal.plus weak mercury caused mental / nervous problems; asc. in gem + mercury in 10H caused headaches, congestion and respiratory diseases; Mercury in dustana is weak constitution, weak nervous system, loss of assets, depression resulting in partial paralysis, stammering,

				disputes connected with property matters, movement to distant places,
Cancer	M	Grace, cleverness, Weak, tender ,mute, fruitful, cancer natives are inconsistent in behaviour, changeable, volatile, relatives and friends near heart, proactive	lungs, chest, ribs, stomach region, breast, vehicular accident, some says heart, sentiments & emotions, behaviour	moon weak and cancer afflicted by malefic then mental problems, weak constitution and body parts indicated,
Leo	L	Vitality, barren, benevolent, progeny, virtues, education	Back, heart, liver and pancreas. black magic, womb / pregnancy, digestive power (pitta), small intestines, procreative power;	if Sun is weak and Leo is afflicted caused vulnerable to the diseases of heart, spine, stomach, etc. and lack stamina and will power. If Sun is strong in 1H caused the person will be noble, generous, and majestic looking . If Sun in 3H caused weak digestions, asthma If Sun in dustana then lack of vitality
Virgo	L	Power of discrimination & analysis,	Waist, abdominal umbilical region, bowel and intestines colon. Nervous system, (vata energy).	Mercury strong caused attractive and charming person; Mercury weak/ debilitated/ combust /in dustana caused prominent veins, lack charm and wit. Mercury and Virgo weak and afflicted caused nervous breakdown, appendicitis, constipation etc..
Libra	L	Talkative, sense of justice, clarity, strong will power, optimism, highly sensitive	Lower abdomen, lumbar region and bones, skin, kidneys, . Semen, Female organs & diseases,	Venus is weak and libra is afflicted then diabetes, venereal diseases, arthritis, gout pains, skin diseases, etc. results. Venus

			varies, Urinary, Female,	strong and well-placed caused attractive personality, charming, smiling nature
Scorpio	L	Mutes, violent, fruitful, severe sentiments, secrets, forceful or unnatural sex	Urinary, anus, generative male organs, bladder, nasal organs and pelvic bones, Anus, Menstruation, infections. Sacrum (kundalini, Sexual vitality)	If Mars is weak and Scorpio is afflicted caused piles, hernia, urinary infections and boils, operations, etc., in the parts ruled by this sign.
Sagittarius	M	Impressive personality, adviser, pleasant nature, analytical bent of mind	Hips and thighs (fat places), arterial system and nerves	Jupiter strong is good health; Jupiter is weak and Sagittarius is afflicted is anaemia, poor digestion, jaundice, high fevers, cold, diabetes, etc...
Capricorn	M	Signifies tact, cheating, lethargy, melancholic nature if Saturn is weak	Flesh, knees, bones & joins, knee caps, especially. (vata flows)	Saturn is weak and Capricorn is afflicted caused joint pains, general weakness, emaciated body, etc.
Aquarius	S	Talkative, from the public, honest, idealistic, sensitive. adverse for longevity when the birth is in twilight.(for native if Aquarius is the 1st house)	Exhaling, skin, calves, Ankles, blood circulation, shim bone, etc. Shanks, Legs, Left ear	Saturn is weak and Aquarius is afflicted caused fractures in legs, wounds, etc., in the parts ruled by this sign
Pisces	S	Enjoyments, sensitiveness, adverse for longevity when the birth is in twilight.(for native if Pisces is the first house)	Feet / toes and their bones, lymphatic system, left eye. (kapha)	if Jupiter and Pisces are afflicted caused diseases to the corresponding parts

Note:

[01] Spine given karaka element to Sun but its governance given to 3-7-11 H together and sign is Aquarius. Some says that Spine ruled by Saturn and its sign is Leo. Personal view is to see 3-7-11 house and sign [Leo] together to see the spine as whole and its karaka is Sun. Nakstras are Punervasu-1 beginning part of spine, Vishakha-1 back bone vertebrae and Purvabhadrapada-1 spine ends. Magha nakstra and Leo sign is spinal cord. Some says Mars nakstra in 3-7-11 sign is the Spinal cord. Pushya is sclerosis.

Let us see the modern medical astrology approach towards the signs rules Bones etc. as per following tabulation.

Sign	Bones	Muscles	Arteries	Veins	Cell Salt
Aries	Cranium & Face	Frontals, occipitals, attolens, deprimens, articularum, zygomaticus, temporal and buccinators	Temporal and internal carotids	The cephalic veins	Kali phos phor ic
Taurus	Cervical vertebrae	Sternohyoid, mastoid, trapezius, sternomastoids, esophagus, stylopheringaeus, splenius and complexes, longus, scalenus, biventres, cervicis, spnals cervicis	External carotids,	Occipital, Jugulars and the veins of thyroid gland	Natr um sulp uricu m
Gemini	Calvicle, scapula, humerus, radius	Deltoid, biceps, supinator, radii sub-clavians, triceps, serratus anticus	Subclavian, brachials,rig ht & left bronechials,	Pulmonary, basilica, subclavians, azygos,	Kali muri aticu m

	ulna, carpal, metacarpal bones and upper ribs	minor, pectorials and palmaris	intercostals, radials and ulnas	veins of the thymus, mediastinum	
Cancer	Sternum, ensiform, cartilage, and part of the ribs,	Diaphragm and intercostals	Auxiliary, diaphragmatic, posterior mediastines, esophagians,	diaphragmatic, gastric, gastroepiploic, mammary	Calcarea fluorica
Leo	Dorsal Vertebrae,	Longissimus and latissumus dorsi, transversalis, diaphragm, heart muscles,	Aorta, anterior and posterior coronary	Vena cava and coronaries,	Magnesia phosphoric
Virgo	None	Obliquus, transversalis of abdomen, rectus pyramidalis,	Gastric, superior and inferior mesenteries	Portal, hepatics, umbilical and intestinal	Kali sulpuricum
Libra	Lumbar vertebrae	Quadrates lumborum and scarolumbars,	Suprarenal, renal and lumbar	Renal and lumbar	Natrum phosphoricum
Scorpio	Tuberosity of ischium, brim of pelvis and symphysis pubis	Cremasterst sphinster, levators, penis, clitoris and sphincter of bladder	Internal iliac	Spermatic, mesenteric, colic, haemorrhoidal	Calcarea sulphuric
Sagittarius	Ilium, femur, coccygeal and sacral	Iliopsoas, iliacus, pectineus, Sartorius, rectus, quadriceps, extensor and gluteus muscles forming the buttocks	External iliac, femoral and sacral	Vena sacra, iliacs and great saphenous	Silicea
Capricorn	Patella	Patellar ligament and popliteus	The iliac and popliteal [to a partial extent]	Poplitea and exterior saphenous	Calcarea phosphoric
Aquarius	Tibia, fibula and inner	Tibialis anticus, peronaeus tertius,	Tibial	Internal saphenous	Natrum

	outer ankles	Achilles tendon, gastrocnemius and soleus			muriaticum
Pisces	Tarsus, metatarsus and phalanges	Short extensor of toes, short flexor of toes, abductor or great and little toes, short flexor of great tie and accessory flexor of toes	Internal and external plantars, tarsal and metatarsal,	Of the feet	Ferrum phosphate

Asterisms attributes and significations

Nakshtra - Element Earth,water, Fire, air,sky	Ruler, Lord, Direction Birth planet*	Sex & Nadi	Body part	Sickness [synchronise with planet, house, affliction etc]	Features Behaviour & tendency [synchronise with planet, house, affliction, benefice etc]	Caste, vowel , Mukha
1 Aswini Earth	Ketu, Aswini Devta N/E	Male , Vata [windy]	Upper Feet The knees	The passage of nose, nostrils, smell, breathings Periodical fever. Or Brain/head problems, meningitis, paralytic stroke, coma, nerves, headache, mental illness, epilepsy, fainting, malaria/ smallpox. Deteriorating health in pada 3	Accomplishing wonderful deeds, Asvini [from Asva-horse] is the power that sets one in motion. Impulsive, aggressive, stubborn, arrogant, over lusty/ over passion, lack discretion;	Xatriya चु, चे, चा, ला cu, ce, cā, lā tiryaka much [slant or horizontal facing]
Bharani Earth	Venus, Yama, N/E Rahu*	Female Pitta [bile]	Toe, Soles, Hips, Loins	Many diseases/ dysentery. Or mucus, catarrh, problems with reproductive organs/ venereal diseases, eyes, forehead. Despondent and inferiority complex in pada 2	Will power, moral duty, self control, discipline, Feeling oppressed, fanatical, intolerant, Struggle, suffering, restraint/ prison/ confinement, irritable / impatient, extreme, narcissism, pride / arrogance, sex indulge. Bearing in womb ,	Xatriya ली, लु, ले, लो lī, lu, le, lo Adhomukha [face downwards]
Krittika earth	Sun, Agni Devta, Local [surrounding all direction]	Female Khafa [phelgam]	Head	Intestinal problems like constipation/ diarrhea. Or cuts, wounds, explosions, sore throat problems, larynx, neck. Bilious indigestion, it may be fire of	Luster and glow of power, full of warmth and feelings [Vrishabha & Shukra], Stubborn, aggressive, fiery emotions, illicit	1 Xatriya 3 Vaishya ई, ऊ, ए, ओ ī, ū, e, o

	Moon*			stomach, body and mind; Mesha & Mangal; skin problems, white-black-red spots	affairs ; a discipline of our desires is required here. Frequent ups and down in life; fame, leather, bestowal wealth, mother noursing	Adhomukha [face downwards]
Rohini Earth	Moon, Prajapati Brahma] Local [surrounding all direction] Moon*	Female Khafa [phelgam	Fore head Throat	Fragnent or perfume or floral allergy; Piles (or rectal disorders). Or cough in pada1, otherwise throat problems, tonsillitis, neck, irregular menses, sunstroke, and obesity.	Rising, birth-generation, growing up, promotion development, cow-cattle, Indulgence in materialism, possessiveness, sensory attachments, infatuation/ losing our soul, jealousy , short temper, stubborn,	Vaishya ओ, वा, वी, वु o, vā, vī, vu Urdhvamukha [face upward]
Mrigasira Earth	Mars, Soma devta, Local [surrounding all direction]	Napushanka, Pitta [bile]	Eyes brose, sight,	Indigestion. Or in pada 1 -2 is larynx, palate, carotid arteries, jugular veins, sore throat, tonsillitis, voice. in pada 3-4 is thymus, arms, itches, fracture, femur, sciatica, trouble in privatise, fever. intestinal channel/tubes,	To ask a girl for marriage, holiness, solicit, reach, journey, investigate, examination, Craving for sensation, indulgence in pleasures (chasing a golden dear) fickle mind. Adorn, to purify, tracing out, range,	2-vaishya 2-shudra वे, वो, का, की ve, vo, kā, kī tiryaka mukh [slant or horizontal
Ardra Water	Rahu, Redra Devta East	Female Vata [windy]	Eyes Throat Dif opine-Hairs, head covered by hair, skull	Weak digestion, all urethral diseases in man and uterus in female. Or in pada 1 is sexual habits. In pada 3 is Laziness. Otherwise Eyes, ears, shoulder, asthma, allergy, mental or nerves disorder.	Abuse of power, egoistic, ungrateful, lusty, greedy, can become proud/violent; wet, moist, grief, pain, squeeze, crush, surpass, overcome, crying, dreadful, hunter, greedy, cruel, sun rays, sun heat	Shudra कु, घ, क, छ ku, gha, ka, cha Urdhvamukh [face upward]
Punarvasu Water	Jupiter, Aditi Devta, East	Male Vata [windy]	Nose Navel	Cholera, indigestion, headache, eye troubles. or pada 1-2-3 is bronchitis, shoulder plates, pulmonary problems, veins, swelling. Pada 4 is nervous problems;	Adobe, restoration, immaterialness, back home, free, safety, infinity, external expanse ; Critical,/careful about the way you speak, over intellectual / and nihilistic, mental	3-shudra 1-Brahman के, को, हा, ही ke, ko, hā, hī Tiryak [slant or

					vacillation, easily pleased and irritated.	horizonta l
Pushya Water	Saturn, Brihaspat i Devta East	Male Pitta [Bile- acidic]	Face, Hips	Tastelessness, Tuberculosis, gastric ulcer, ulceration in respiratory system, cough, gallstones, nausea, belching, obstruction, bruises in the breast, cancer, phthisis, sclerosis jaundice, hiccups, pyorrhoea, eczema;.pada 1is hypersensitive, pada 2 is coughing. Or lips / mouth/ ears diseases, hip cup.	Stubborn, selfish, arrogant, jealous, quickly deflated by criticism. The best of upper most of anything, light, lustre, brittiance, a Nobel man, wise and old man, most respectable, strong, powerful, gladden, to give, liberal, munificent, elders, ancestors, pro-generators of mankind, giving or owning great prosperity , perfection,	Brahman हु, हे, हो, डा hu, he, ho, ḍā Urdhvam ukh [face upward]
Ashlesh a Water	Mercury, Sarpa Devta, *Ketu S/E	Femal e kapha	Ears Left Foot, nails	Anemia. Poor or bad / unhealthy diet, indigestion, food poisoning, liver, oesophagus, pancreas/ diaphragm, lips, nails, pain in legs and knees, nervous problems/very sensitive/ psychic. Pda 2 is weak health.	Nervous system over sensitive, cannot tolerate humiliation or criticism, mental instability, cold – blooded ,worry, fear, melancholy, tendency to lie/deceptive, difficulty to control our diet, pain is inevitable, suffering is optional. Cannot control the tongue.	Brahman डी, डु, डे, डो ḍī, ḍu, ḍe, ḍo Adhomuk ha [face downwar ds]
Magha Water	Ketu, Pitru Deva, *Venus S/E	Femal e Kafa	Lips & Chins Feet, nose	Neck, chin, lips, heart, back, spinal cord, spleen, dorsal region of spine, aorta, Diseases: Heart affected by sudden shock, grief, poison, backache, cholera, humors, gravel in kidney, palpitation, regurgitation, Fainting; spinal	Racial superiority, identification with class status, pride, arrogance, can win a kingdom but lose his soul, sensual allurements.	Xatriya मा, मी, मू, मे mā, mī, mū, me Adhomuk ha [face downwar ds]

				meningitis, Breathing problem / respiratory system; pada 1 is trouble from excess of sex . pada 4 is overeating. Otherwise nose, neck, spinal cord, spleen, aorta, shock of heart, grief, palpitations, hypertension, heart problems.		
Purva Falguni Water	Venus, Arynmna Devta *Jupiter S/E	Femal e Pitta	Right Hand Hip II Lips, sex organs	cough (dry or wet). Heart swelling/ blood pressure, lips, shoulders, addiction to sex, disappointment in love, spine bent, anaemia, pain in legs, feet swelling, fire accidents, Gout-Lumbago-sciatica; pada- 4 is boils and ulcers.	Dispenser, fulfilment, attainment, rejection of evil-bad, cleansing, refinement, split, burst, feel, to bring to maturity, cultivate. Craving for timulation, sensual pleasures, narcissism, indulgence, vanity, black magic etc.. Fond of sweets and fond of eating. Prolific nature	Xatriya मो, टा, टी, टृ mo, ṭā, ṭī, ṭṛ Adhomuk ha [face downwar ds]
Uttara Falguni Fire	Sun, Bhaga Devta *Jupiter Soth	Femal e Vata	Left Hand Navel II forehea d	Skin disease. Intestinal disorder, tumor in bowels, liver, stomach disorder, swelling neck, left-hand, sore throat, blood pressure/ palpitations, blood clotting in head; craziness. pada 1 is Spotted fever, plague, pains in the back and head, hyperemia, blood pressure, fainting, Back ache, temporary madness caused by clotting of blood in brain capillaries, palpitation. pada 2 is bad health. For Pada 2 3 and 4 Human Body: Intestines, bowels, liver. Diseases: Fainting, palpitation, stomach disorder,	Conspicuous, variegated, speckled, agitated, illusion, unreality, wonder, dazzling; picture, delineation, heaped. Deep sense of loneliness is there is no good relationships, desiring to control authors with mystic practices / tantra / magic etc.. tendency to be over giving then feel the ingratitude of others.	1-Xatriya 3-Vaishya टे, टो, पा, पी ṭe, ṭo, pā, pī Urdhvam ukh [face upward]

				swelling in neck, tumours in the bowels, sore throat		
Hasta Fire	Moon, Surya Devta South	Male Vata	Fingers Throat	Diabetes. Vitamin 'B' deficiency, flatulence, gas formation, loose bowels, pain & disorder in the bowels, worms, dysentery, mucus, weak arms & shoulders, short breath, fear complex, hysteria, diarrheal, typhoid, cholera, neuralgia ,jaundice - skin troubles, pada 3 is worries, sensitiveness.	Become impatient/ critical under stress, can become cunning/Merciless / thieving, need some peace and very nature to revitalize. Cannot support alcohol or drugs.	Vaishya पू, प, ण, ठ pū, pa, ṇa, ṭha tiryaka mukh [slant or horizonta l
Chitra Fire	Mars, Tvashtra Devta South	Femal e Ptta	Neck Forehe ad	Dizziness/ loss of conciousness.. pada 1 and 2 is wounds from insects/ reptiles, or in Lower parts ulcers / Pains / itching/ worms . Pada 3 and 4 is loins/ lumbago/ kidney problems, spine, vasodilatation, appendicitis, urethra, inflammation, hernia, sunstroke, brain fever / headache.	Represents regenerative power and longevity.	2- Vaishya 2-Shudra पे, पो, रा, री pe, po, rā, rī tiryaka mukh [slant or horizonta l
Swati Fire	Rahu Vaayu Devta S/W	Femal e Kafa	Chest; Heart-Soul Pranav ayu [oxyge n] Throat, Teeth II Stomac h, bowels, womb	eye diseases. Stomach / intestinal gas problems / flatulence / appendicitis / hernia, bladder/blood in urine / kidney inflammation, skin roblems/eczema. pada 1 or 2is irritable, hot temper, epileptic	Air, sensibility, awakened consciousness, self-own like self moving-supporting etc., agreeing, signal, , strong lust for life and financial success, restlessness / discontent, self centred for profits, scatter and move things around. Cannot tolerate criticism, cannot decide.	Shudra रु, रे, रो, ता ru, re, ro, tā tiryaka mukh [slant or horizonta l
Visakha Fire	Jupiter Indraagni Devta *Sun S/E	Femal e Kaph a	Breast lungs Navel, arms	ear diseases, headache fever .pada 1,2 and 3 is lower stomach, abdomen, pancreas, organs near	Over ambitious, aggressive, dictatorial, angry, quarrelsome, envious of other's	3-Shudra 1- Brahman ती, तू, ते,

				bladder, renal abscess, adrenalin, diabetics, skin eruption , vertigo/ coma. Pada 4 is urethra, bladder, prostate, rectum, colon, womb, menses, nose bleeding, kidneys stones.	achievements, bitterness if isolated, over sex drive / infidelity.	तो tī, tū, te, to Adhomukh [face downwards]
Anuradha Fire	Saturn Mitra Devta *Sun S/E	Male Pitta	Stomach Hip	nose problems. Otherwise stomach, womb, bowels, intestine , breasts , rectum, piles, bladder, nasal bones, pelvic bones , suppression of menses/ severe pain , constipation, sterility, catarrh from nose, fracture of hip bone. testicles of Visvarupa	Low tolerance level = frustration / melancholy because of lack of Affection / or mother, jealousy / desire to control others, pitfalls and hardships in early life, strong appetite for life.	Brahman ना, नी, नु, ने nā, nī, nu, ne tiryaka mukh [slant or horizontal
Jyestha Air	Mercury Indra Devta West	Female Vata	Trunk Right Side Feet II Middlefinger, neck, nape	diseases of the mouth/ teeth & gums / tongue / upper lips / throat / neck, or nave l, upper limbs, ovaries, genitals, colon , or pain in back neck/ears/arms/shoulders. right side of the torso	Eldest, senior, selfish, chief, praised glorified, Arrogance, pride, anything preferred; seclusion, secretive, irritable, impatience, fall from grace/ opulences. Brings sorrow and poverty if the star is unfavorable.	Brahman नो, य, यी, यु no, ya, yī, yu tiryaka mukh [slant or horizontal
Mula Air	Ketu Niruti Devta West	Napushak Vata	Trunk Left Side Feet	Tuberculosis. Trunk/torso left side, testicles, femur, ileum/last part of the small intestine, sciatic nerves, hips, Inability to coordinate muscle movements; unsteady movements and staggering gait, lumbago. left ear; micro organisms/ germs/viruses (ketu lord). Diseases: Rheumatism, pulmonary troubles , Hip and thigh problems, Sciatic nerve troubles, Foot problems, Obesity, liver issues, Mental vacillation, femur, lumbago	Idea of origin, origin foundation, Root cause in science, philosophy, any knowledge, religious, Moxa; chief, capital; pain is inevitable, suffering is optional. Cleverness, suspicion, bold , investigating. violence and cruelty. Arrogance, egotism, lust and anger can be experienced here. the pain is intended to set the person on the right track	Xatriya ये, यो, भा, भी ye, yo, bhā, bhī Adhomukh [face downwards]

PurvaShad Air	Venus Varuna Devta *Mars West	Female Pitta	Back below waist Hip	Left side of Virat-rupa + Thighs of naksatra purusa. Bladder and kidney problems/ stones. Otherwise Right thigh, sex organs diseases, coccyx, iliac artery (end of aorta, pelvis low region), sciatica, diabetes, rheumatism, gout, respiratory diseases/lung cancer/cold problems, blood putrefaction.	Never submit, obstinate, independent, do not consider other's opinions, over egoistic, expansive.	Xatriya भु, धा, फ़ा, ढा bhu, dhā, phaā, Dhā Adhomukh [face downwards]
Uttraashada Air	Sun Vishvedeva *Mars N/E	Female Kafa		Left nostril, thighs, Beware of; eye troubles - disorders of limbs - consumption - gout - toothache. Vomiting. pada 1 is femur, sciatica , limb paralysis, affection of the eyes, pulmonary diseases . Padas 2,3 and 4 is knee cap , eczema, dry skin disease/inflammation , leprosy, bone problems, dull pain, digestive trouble, stomach gas, heart palpitation	Total is involvement in something ,idealists/ deep humanitarian concern, Stubborn, self-centered, lazy, Apathy.	1-Xatriya 3-Vaishya भे, भो, जा, जी bhe, bho, jā, jī Urdhvamukh [face upward
Shravana Air	Moon Vishnu Devta *Mercury N/E	Male Kafa	Genitals Throat / neck	Body below Navel, calves, knee, skin, lymphatic vessels . right eye of virata rupa; Ears (& equilibrium); tastelessness. Poor digestion, skin diseases, pus/boils, tuberculosis/ pleurisy, rheumatism.	Progress, to hear, listen, attentive, obedient, intellectual pursuits, celebrity, news, words, knowledge; disciple, teacher, stream, passage of urine, deportment; Disillusioned early in life, easily hurt by others opinions, make and listen to gossips (prajalpa), rigid / obstinate, jealous of enemies. Children bring trouble and anxiety.	Vaishya खी, खू, खे, खो khī, khū, khe, kho Urdhvamukh [face upward
Dhanista Ether/space	Mars Asta Vasu Devta *Mercury	Female Pitta	Anus Sex organs Head	Thighs, Back (kundalini), hip joint, right ear, Pains caused by vata disorders ; twist of	In Makar river and in Kumbha sea; delayed or unhappy marriage; singing, accents, melody	2-Vaishya 2-Shudra गा, गी, गू,

	N/E		II Back	ligaments/ rheumatism etc.,high fever /malaria , elephantiasis. pada 1 and 2 indicates knee cap, jail. Dry cough, hiccups, leucocytes in blood, gout, boils, lameness, amputation, injury in the leg. Padas 3 and 4 is ankles, tibia/peronea, fracture of legs, blood poisoning / high-pressure/ varicose/ overheated blood, fainting.	music, wealth & riches, distilling, perspiration, wet, moisture;.. Lack patience perseverance in face of problems, greedy, stingy, strive to acquire by any means / covet other's wealth. money,, power, influence, don't like to be commended, bold, brave, stubborn	गे gā, gī, gū, ge Urdhvam ukh [face upward
Satabhis ha Ether/sp ace	Rahu Varuna North	Napu shak Vata	Right Thigh Throat , neck II Jaws	Peroneous / Achilles tendon, calf muscle, Jaws (eat / drink/ speak), back of thighs; Right Thigh, right shoulder, Laughter, Bilous diseases. Arthritis/ rheumatism, ankles/ calves, hypertension / palpitation, jaw problems, insomnia, fracture of bones, eczema. Guinea worms.	Healer, physicial, medical man, SomaRasa [spiritual liquor; to conceal hide, ward off, prohibit; covered-surrounded, hindering; water place, protector from evil, defence; shield, clad, dropsy paralysis, incurable disease; share, trap; Depressed / lonely / restricted by duty, unstable childhood is expected because the period of Rahu starts. hard to convince. Any planets here will make its house losing its karakas. Satabhisha brings invariably mental pain	Shudra गो, सा, सी, सू go, sā, sī, sū Urdhvam ukh [face upward
Purvabh adrapad a Ether / Space	Jupiter Ajaikpad a Devta North	Male Vata	Left Thigh Navel Ii Region of the ribs,	Soles of feet, unless, legs, right flanks, Ribs. Phlegmatic disease, Irregularity of circulative system, ulcerated gums, mottled/spotted tooth enamel. Or pada 1 2 and 3 is swollen ankles, dilated heart, ulcers, blood pressure, apoplexy, enlarged liver, ribs, injuries from fall down accidents or attacks. Pada 4 is	Sense of cruelty, burn, punish, to torture, to undergo penance, self-mortification, destroy, perish, pain, grief; Over critical/ over idealistic, coerce to convince others of their ideals, very nervous and worrisome if in stress, angry, impulsive, anxious,	3-Shudra 1-Brahman से, सो, दा, दी se, so, dā, dī Urdhvam ukh [face upward

				Toes, perspiring feet, swelling in feet, enlarged liver, jaundice, hernia, sprue, corns in feet, intestines affected, abdominal tumor/ pain.	cynical. Intense internal purification, very impetuous mind immensely active with courage and detachment, will suffer anguish and sorrow if selfishness is there.	
Uttrabhadrapada Ether/space	Saturn Ahirbudhnya Devta North	Male Pitta	Shin / Tibia ankle Hip	the right side/ flank / ribs, diseases due to fatigue. foot problems/ fracture/ cold feet, indigestion/ constipation/ flatulence/ liver problem, swelling because of serum fluid, determination and perseverance, stress, disorder. Except in pada 4 is weak mind.	Power to control and endurance, journey to distant place; renunciation, wondering, wisdom or qualitative disposal; Very strong character when material goals are involved. Gives bad judgment. Gives prosperity with patience, self-discipline, tolerate pain, renounced, love seclusion.	Brahman दू ज्ञा झा था dū jñā jhā thā Urdhvamukh [face upward
Revati Ether/space	Mercury Pusha Devta N/E	Female Kafa	Ankles Feet II Cavity Of abdomen	Abdominal cavity, navel (Manipur chakra), toes. Diseases developed from boils and wounds. Intestinal ulcers, abdominal disorder/ stomach problems, deformities of the feet, gout, cramps, lassitude, inflammation of the kidney, deafness, pus in ears. Childhood sickness especially if Revati is afflicted , insomnia, nightmares, sensitive nervous system.	Nursing and feeding; infantile & child disease & death; develop, unfold, time, finality, finish,; Paediatric / childhood diseases, low self-esteem, inferiority complex, can become hard template and stubborn if provoked. Over generous, over sensitive to harsh reality. Loud voice, most clever, and tricky, able to charm completely others, perfection of sociability Talents, Intuition, previous life memory or intuition	Brahman दे दो चा ची de do cā cī tiryaka mukh [slant or horizontal

- * Certain planets and constellation are similar in nature and those nakstras are called the birth nakstra [janma nakstra] of that Graham. If janama nakstra of planet is occupied by another planet it will alter the nature – fetures of corresponding planet.

How to use this attributes and significations depends on the expertise and experience of the astrologer.
Suppose Taurus is the ascendant, Saturn retro there at 13.04 degree with Mandi / Gulika, receiving Rahu aspect. 1H is general physique and Saturn-Mandi there may give sick and ailed body or periodical sufferings. 1H is also brain and take Rahu aspect there means chronic or non-curable disease of body or brain. 3H has Ketu and aspect of Saturn, Rahu, and Mars and suppose Pushya nakstra is most afflicted then Sclerosis [pushya] of spine [3H] and brain [1H] is possible. If Rahu, Mars, or both also afflict Chandra and Venus, the disease will be more prolonged, acute and sever.

Chapter-12
Higher Division scheme

Shastyamsa [D60], khavedamsa [D40] and axavedamsa [D45] varga [division] scheme

These divisions shall be used for the assessment of most afflicted star in the chart as said in previous chapter/s.

Khavedamsa [D40- division fortieth]

Here in this scheme, there are forty divisions of thirty degree of a sign, each division comprises of 00.45 degree. In odd sign the division started from Aries [1] and even sign it is from Libra [7] and is carried forward in the same order like 1,2,3,4...12,1,2,3...in continuation till the 40th part and similarly from Libra in continuation till the end. The lord of the divisions are in repeated form of order is Vishnu, Chandra, Marichi, Tavsta, Dhata, Shiva, Ravi, Yama, Yaxes, Gandharva, Kala and Varuna.
The scheme is tabulated as below.

In the example [01] female chart of Ch-13, it is 03.43 degree of Gemini is afflicted then as per the scheme depicted in the table below it comes to 5th part of D40, which is Leo sign where Saturn is posited. And if we consider independent aspect of divisional chart then Sun is under Rahu, Saturn, Mars aspect and Sun being natural karaka of physique, Brain-head the female is insane and its is mental aberration or bipolar disorder case.

Sr No	Lord	Sign 1	Sign 2	Sign 3	Sign 4	5	6	7	8	9	10	11	12	Amsa
01	Vishnu	1	7	1	7	1	7	1	7	1	7	1	7	00.45
02	Chndra	2	8	2	8	2	8	2	8	2	8	2	8	01.30
03	Marichi	3	9	3	9	3	9	3	9	3	9	3	9	02.15
04	Tvasta	4	10	4	10	4	10	4	10	4	10	4	10	03.00
05	Dhata	5	11	5	11	5	11	5	11	5	11	5	11	03.45
06	Shiva	6	12	6	12	6	12	6	12	6	12	6	12	04.30
07	Ravi	7	1	7	1	7	1	7	1	7	1	7	1	05.15
08	Yama	8	2	8	2	8	2	8	2	8	2	8	2	06.00
09	Yaxes	9	3	9	3	9	3	9	3	9	3	9	3	06.45
10	Gandhrv	10	4	10	4	10	4	10	4	10	4	10	4	07.30
11	Kala	11	5	11	5	11	5	11	5	11	5	11	5	08.15
12	Varuna	12	6	12	6	12	6	12	6	12	6	12	6	09.00
13	Vishnu	1	7	1	7	1	7	1	7	1	7	1	7	09.45
14	Chndra	2	8	2	8	2	8	2	8	2	8	2	8	10.30
15	Marichi	3	9	3	9	3	9	3	9	3	9	3	9	11.15
16	Tvasta	4	10	4	10	4	10	4	10	4	10	4	10	12.00
17	Dhata	5	11	5	11	5	11	5	11	5	11	5	11	12.45
18	Shiva	6	12	6	12	6	12	6	12	6	12	6	12	13.30
19	Ravi	7	1	7	1	7	1	7	1	7	1	7	1	14.15
20	Yama	8	2	8	2	8	2	8	2	8	2	8	2	15.00
21	Yaxes	9	3	9	3	9	3	9	3	9	3	9	3	15.45
22	Gandh	10	4	10	4	10	4	10	4	10	4	10	4	16.30

	arv													
23	Kala	11	5	11	5	11	5	11	5	11	5	11	5	17.15
24	Varuna	12	6	12	6	12	6	12	6	12	6	12	6	18.00
25	Vishnu	1	7	1	7	1	7	1	7	1	7	1	7	18.45
26	Chndra	2	8	2	8	2	8	2	8	2	8	2	8	19.30
27	Marichi	3	9	3	9	3	9	3	9	3	9	3	9	20.15
28	Tvasta	4	10	4	10	4	10	4	10	4	10	4	10	21.00
29	Dhata	5	11	5	11	5	11	5	11	5	11	5	11	21.45
30	Shiva	6	12	6	12	6	12	6	12	6	12	6	12	22.30
31	Ravi	7	1	7	1	7	1	7	1	7	1	7	1	23.15
32	Yama	8	2	8	2	8	2	8	2	8	2	8	2	24.00
33	Yaxes	9	3	9	3	9	3	9	3	9	3	9	3	24.45
34	Gandharv	10	4	10	4	10	4	10	4	10	4	10	4	25.30
35	Kala	11	5	11	5	11	5	11	5	11	5	11	5	26.15
36	Varuna	12	6	12	6	12	6	12	6	12	6	12	6	27.00
37	Vishnu	1	7	1	7	1	7	1	7	1	7	1	7	27.45
38	Chndra	2	8	2	8	2	8	2	8	2	8	2	8	28.30
39	Marichi	3	9	3	9	3	9	3	9	3	9	3	9	29.15
40	Tvasta	4	10	4	10	4	10	4	10	4	10	4	10	30.00

Axavedamsa [D45 – division forty-fifth]

Here in this scheme, there are forty five divisions of thirty degree of a sign, each division comprises of 00.40 degree.

In moveable sign the division started from Aries [1], immovable sign it is from Leo [5] and in the dual sign it is from Sagittarius [9] is carried forward in the same order like 1,2,3,4…12…1,2,3…in continuation till the 45th part and similarly from Leo and Sagittarius in continuation till the end.

The lord of the divisions are in repeated form of order is Brahma, Vishnu, Shankar [Br-Vi-Sh] for moveable sign, Shankar, Vishnu Brahma [Sh-Vi-Br] for immovable sign and Vishnu, Brahma, Shankar [Vi-Br-Sh] for dual sign.

The scheme is tabulated as below.

Sr No	Lord Br-Vi-Sh Aries 1	Sh-Vi-Br Taurs 2	Vi-Br-Sh Gemini 3	Ca 4	Le 5	Vi 6	Li 7	Sc 8	Sa 9	Cp 10	Aq 11	Pi 12	Amsa Degree
01	1	5	9	1	5	9	1	5	9	1	5	9	00.40
02	2	6	10	2	6	10	2	6	10	2	6	10	01.20
03	3	7	11	3	7	11	3	7	11	3	7	11	02.00
04	4	8	12	4	8	12	4	8	12	4	8	12	02.40
05	5	9	1	5	9	1	5	9	1	5	9	1	03.20
06	6	10	2	6	10	2	6	10	2	6	10	2	04.00
07	7	11	3	7	11	3	7	11	3	7	11	3	04.40
08	8	12	4	8	12	4	8	12	4	8	12	4	05.20
09	9	1	5	9	1	5	9	1	5	9	1	5	06.00
10	10	2	6	10	2	6	10	2	6	10	2	6	06.40
11	11	3	7	11	3	7	11	3	7	11	3	7	07.20
12	12	4	8	12	4	8	12	4	8	12	4	8	08.00
13	1	5	9	1	5	9	1	5	9	1	5	9	08.40
14	2	6	10	2	6	10	2	6	10	2	6	10	09.20
15	3	7	11	3	7	11	3	7	11	3	7	11	10.00
16	4	8	12	4	8	12	4	8	12	4	8	12	10.40
17	5	9	1	5	9	1	5	9	1	5	9	1	11.20
18	6	10	2	6	10	2	6	10	2	6	10	2	12.00
19	7	11	3	7	11	3	7	11	3	7	11	3	12.40
20	8	12	4	8	12	4	8	12	4	8	12	4	13.20
21	9	1	5	9	1	5	9	1	5	9	1	5	14.00

22	10	2	6	10	2	6	10	2	6	10	2	6	14.40
23	11	3	7	11	3	7	11	3	7	11	3	7	15.20
24	12	4	8	12	4	8	12	4	8	12	4	8	16.00
25	1	5	9	1	5	9	1	5	9	1	5	9	16.40
26	2	6	10	2	6	10	2	6	10	2	6	10	17.20
27	3	7	11	3	7	11	3	7	11	3	7	11	18.00
28	4	8	12	4	8	12	4	8	12	4	8	12	18.40
29	5	9	1	5	9	1	5	9	1	5	9	1	19.20
30	6	10	2	6	10	2	6	10	2	6	10	2	20.00
31	7	11	3	7	11	3	7	11	3	7	11	3	20.40
32	8	12	4	8	12	4	8	12	4	8	12	4	21.20
33	9	1	5	9	1	5	9	1	5	9	1	5	22.00
34	10	2	6	10	2	6	10	2	6	10	2	6	22.40
35	11	3	7	11	3	7	11	3	7	11	3	7	23.20
36	12	4	8	12	4	8	12	4	8	12	4	8	24.00
37	1	5	9	1	5	9	1	5	9	1	5	9	24.40
38	2	6	10	2	6	10	2	6	10	2	6	10	25.20
39	3	7	11	3	7	11	3	7	11	3	7	11	26.00
40	4	8	12	4	8	12	4	8	12	4	8	12	26.40
41	5	9	1	5	9	1	5	9	1	5	9	1	27.20
42	6	10	2	6	10	2	6	10	2	6	10	2	28.00
43	7	11	3	7	11	3	7	11	3	7	11	3	28.40
44	8	12	4	8	12	4	8	12	4	8	12	4	29.20
45	9	1	5	9	1	5	9	1	5	9	1	5	30.00

Shastyamsa [D60-division sixtieth]

Here in this division there are sixty parts each part comprises of 00.30 degree out of total 30.00 degree of a sign. The sign of the first part starts from the sign itself like 1,2,3.. to 12 and ends with respective sixtieth part in continuation like 12,1,2,... 11.

Lords of these sixty parts for odd signs are as under and for even signs the order is reversed. Benevolent and Malevolent-cruel part of this division is indicated as

[B] & [M] as under and to avoid double writing the scheme is tabulated below. Best thing for the beginner is to find the D60 sign and its devta from the following table.

Sr No	B/ M	Lord Odd	Lord Even	Sign 1	2	3	4	5	6	7	8	9	10	11	12	Amsh Degr
01	M	Ghora	Indurekha	1	2	3	4	5	6	7	8	9	10	11	12	00.30
02	M	Raxas	Bhraman	2	3	4	5	6	7	8	9	10	11	12	1	01.00
03	B	Deva	Payodhi	3	4	5	6	7	8	9	10	11	12	1	2	01.30
04	B	Kubera	Sudha	4	5	6	7	8	9	10	11	12	1	2	3	02.00
05	M	Yaxa	Atishital	5	6	7	8	9	10	11	12	1	2	3	4	02.30
06	M	Kinnar	Krura	6	7	8	9	10	11	12	1	2	3	4	5	03.00
07	M	Bhrasta	Saumya	7	8	9	10	11	12	1	2	3	4	5	6	03.30
08	M	Kulghna	Nirmal	8	9	10	11	12	1	2	3	4	5	6	7	04.00
09	M	Garala	Dandayudha	9	10	11	12	1	2	3	4	5	6	7	8	04.30
10	M	Agni	Kalagni	10	11	12	1	2	3	4	5	6	7	8	9	05.00
11	M	Maya	Pravin	11	12	1	2	3	4	5	6	7	8	9	10	05.30
12	M	Purisha	Indumukh	12	1	2	3	4	5	6	7	8	9	10	11	06.00
13	B	Apampati	Damstrakarl	1	2	3	4	5	6	7	8	9	10	11	12	06.30
14	B	Marutavt	Shitala	2	3	4	5	6	7	8	9	10	11	12	1	07.00
15	M	Kala	Komal	3	4	5	6	7	8	9	10	11	12	1	2	07.30
16	M	Ahibhaga	Saumya	4	5	6	7	8	9	10	11	12	1	2	3	08.00
17	B	Amruta	Kalarupa	5	6	7	8	9	10	11	12	1	2	3	4	08.30
18	B	Chnadra	Utpata	6	7	8	9	10	11	12	1	2	3	4	5	09.00
19	B	Mrudu	Vamshaxaya	7	8	9	10	11	12	1	2	3	4	5	6	09.30
20	B	Komal	Kulnasha	8	9	10	11	12	1	2	3	4	5	6	7	10.00
21	B	Heramba	Vishpradgdh	9	10	11	12	1	2	3	4	5	6	7	8	10.30
22	B	Brahma	Purnachandr	10	11	12	1	2	3	4	5	6	7	8	9	11.00
23	B	Vishnu	Amruta	11	12	1	2	3	4	5	6	7	8	9	10	11.30
24	B	Maheshvar	Sudhaa	12	1	2	3	4	5	6	7	8	9	10	11	12.00
25	B	Deva	Kantak	1	2	3	4	5	6	7	8	9	10	11	12	12.

			a													30
26	B	Adra	Yama	2	3	4	5	6	7	8	9	10	11	12	1	13.00
27	B	Kalinasha	Ghora	3	4	5	6	7	8	9	10	11	12	1	2	13.30
28	B	Xitishvar	Davagni	4	5	6	7	8	9	10	11	12	1	2	3	14.00
29	B	Kamlakar	Kala	5	6	7	8	9	10	11	12	1	2	3	4	14.30
30	M	Gulika	Mrutyu	6	7	8	9	10	11	12	1	2	3	4	5	15.00
31	M	Mrutyu	Gulika	7	8	9	10	11	12	1	2	3	4	5	6	15.30
32	M	Kala	Kamlakar	8	9	10	11	12	1	2	3	4	5	6	7	16.00
33	M	Davagni	Xitishvar	9	10	11	12	1	2	3	4	5	6	7	8	16.30
34	M	Ghora	Kalinasha	10	11	12	1	2	3	4	5	6	7	8	9	17.00
35	M	Yama	Adra	11	12	1	2	3	4	5	6	7	8	9	10	17.30
36	M	Kantaka	Deva	12	1	2	3	4	5	6	7	8	9	10	11	18.00
37	B	Sudhaa	Maheshvar	1	2	3	4	5	6	7	8	9	10	11	12	18.30
38	B	Amruta	Vishnu	2	3	4	5	6	7	8	9	10	11	12	1	19.00
39	B	Purnachandr	Brahma	3	4	5	6	7	8	9	10	11	12	1	2	19.30
40	M	Vishpradgdh	Heramba	4	5	6	7	8	9	10	11	12	1	2	3	20.00
41	M	Kulnasha	Komal	5	6	7	8	9	10	11	12	1	2	3	4	20.30
42	M	Vamshaxaya	Mrudu	6	7	8	9	10	11	12	1	2	3	4	5	21.00
43	M	Utpata	Chandra	7	8	9	10	11	12	1	2	3	4	5	6	21.30
44	M	Kalarupa	Amruta	8	9	10	11	12	1	2	3	4	5	6	7	22.00
45	B	Saumya	Ahibhaga	9	10	11	12	1	2	3	4	5	6	7	8	22.30
46	B	Komal	Kala	10	11	12	1	2	3	4	5	6	7	8	9	23.00
47	B	Shital	Marutvat	11	12	1	2	3	4	5	6	7	8	9	10	23.30
48	M	Damstrakaral	Apampati	12	1	2	3	4	5	6	7	8	9	10	11	24.00
49	B	Indumukha	Purisha	1	2	3	4	5	6	7	8	9	10	11	12	24.30
50	B	Pravina	Maya	2	3	4	5	6	7	8	9	10	11	12	1	25.00
51	M	Kalagni	Agni	3	4	5	6	7	8	9	10	11	12	1	2	25.30
52	M	Dandayudha	Garala	4	5	6	7	8	9	10	11	12	1	2	3	26.00
53	B	Nirmal	Kulagna	5	6	7	8	9	10	11	12	1	2	3	4	26.30
54	B	Saumya	Bhrasta	6	7	8	9	10	11	12	1	2	3	4	5	27.00
55	M	Krura	Kinnar	7	8	9	10	11	12	1	2	3	4	5	6	27.

																30
56	B	Atishitaal	Yaxa	8	9	10	11	12	1	2	3	4	5	6	7	28.00
57	B	Sudha	Kubera	9	10	11	12	1	2	3	4	5	6	7	8	28.30
58	B	Payodhi	Deva	10	11	12	1	2	3	4	5	6	7	8	9	29.00
59	M	Bhramana	Raxasa	11	12	1	2	3	4	5	6	7	8	9	10	29.30
60	M	Indurekha	Ghora	12	1	2	3	4	5	6	7	8	9	10	11	30.00

Out of the above sixty parts-divisions, 30 parts are cruel and 30 parts are auspicious as natal chart is the imprint of the native who are in equal portion of paapa and punya and to preserve the symmetry this dual category is bifurcated. Each of the amsa in Shashtiamsa is 00:30:00 (30 minutes) duration. So, one can easily see if the amsa is kroora or saumya. The sign lord of amsa reckoned from the sign itself. The following parts of the D60 are malevolent in nature totalling to 30. 1,2,5,6,7,8,9,10,11,12,15,16,30,31,32,33,34,35,36,40,41,42,43,44,48,51,52,55,59,60. The remaining 30 divisions are auspicious in nature.

Chapter - 13

Most Afflicted Mrigsirsha Nakstra

[01] Female-Mnssavpi

Date: April 28, 1977; Time: 6:50:00 am; Time Zone: 5:30:00 (East of GMT); Place: 72 E 54' 00", 20 N 22' 00"; Vapi, India; Nakshatra: Magha (Ke) (90.74% left); Ayanamsa: 23-31-29.42

History & Sufferings: The native has been suffering since last 16/17 years when she left her study from second year of graduation and could not complete the same. She is unmarried and self-talking, anguish, depressed and shouting. This is the acute case of Bipolar disorder. She could not get married.
Bipolar disorder (also known as bipolar affective disorder, manic-depressive disorder, or manic depression) is a mental illness characterized by episodes of an elevated or agitated mood known as mania that often alternates with episodes of depression. These episodes can impair the individual's ability to function in ordinary life. The cause is not clearly understood, but genetic, neurological and environmental risk factors are believed to play a role. This includes Self-talk, Illusions, Dreaming, Mood swings, Depression, Aggression, Obsessive, No interest in work and zero motivation.

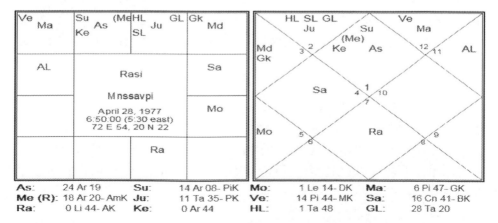

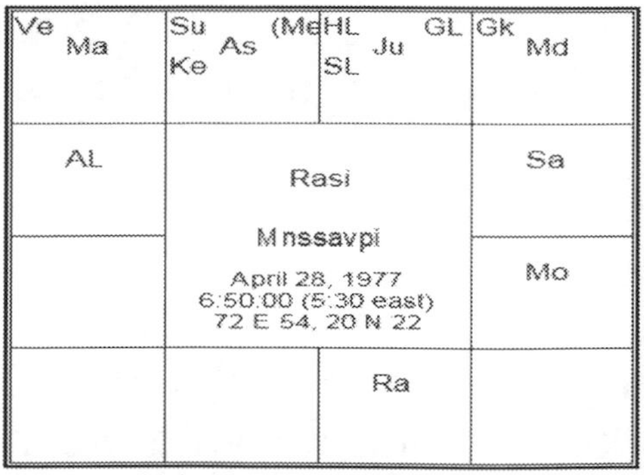

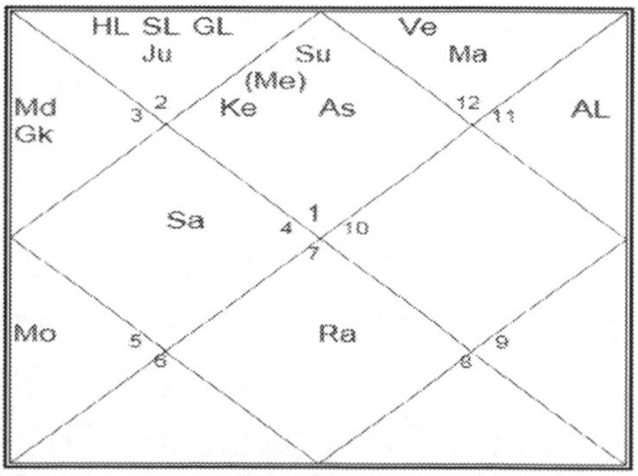

As:	24 Ar 19	**Su**:	14 Ar 08- PiK	**Mo**:	1 Le 14- DK	**Ma**:	6 Pi 47- GK
Me (R):	18 Ar 20- AmK	**Ju**:	11 Ta 35- PK	**Ve**:	14 Pi 44- MK	**Sa**:	16 Cn 41- BK
Ra:	0 Li 44- AK	**Ke**:	0 Ar 44	**HL**:	1 Ta 48	**GL**:	28 Ta 20

Gulika 3Gemini43 degree

D9

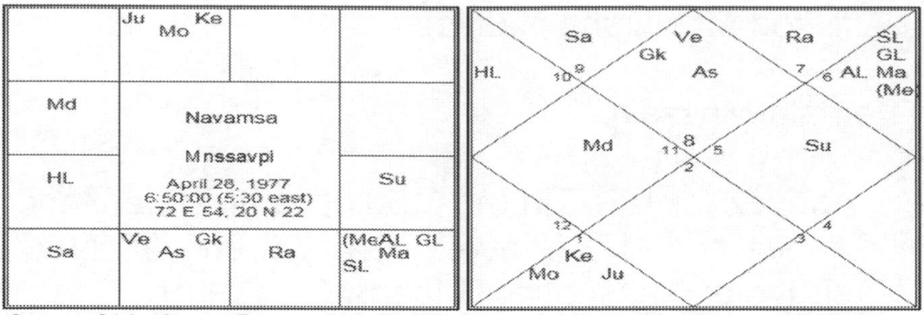

As:	24 Ar 19	Su:	14 Ar 08- PiK	Mo:	1 Le 14- DK	Ma:	6 Pi 47- GK
Me (R):	18 Ar 20- AmK	Ju:	11 Ta 35- PK	Ve:	14 Pi 44- MK	Sa:	16 Cn 41- BK
Ra:	0 Li 44- AK	Ke:	0 Ar 44	HL:	1 Ta 48	GL:	28 Ta 20

D40

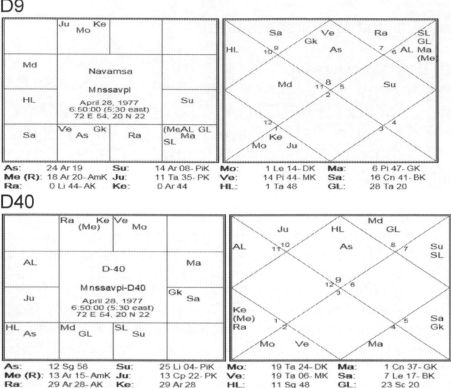

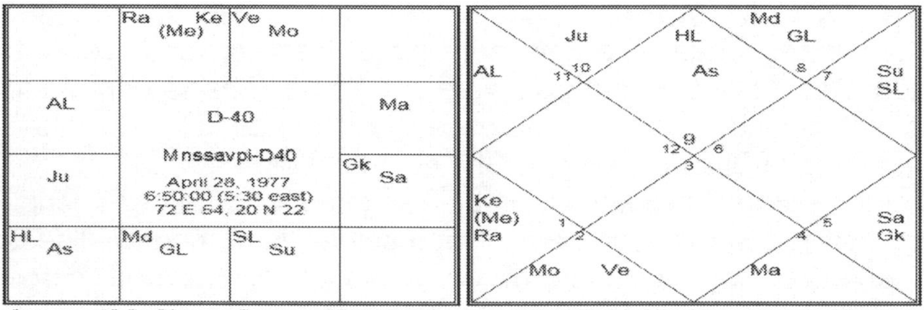

As:	12 Sg 58	Su:	25 Li 04- PiK	Mo:	19 Ta 24- DK	Ma:	1 Cn 37- GK
Me (R):	13 Ar 15- AmK	Ju:	13 Cp 22- PK	Ve:	19 Ta 06- MK	Sa:	7 Le 17- BK
Ra:	29 Ar 28- AK	Ke:	29 Ar 28	HL:	11 Sg 48	GL:	23 Sc 20

[01] Most afflicted Nakstra with round about 3.00-degree orbs of Mars & Rahu

Gulika at 3Gemini43" with Rahu and Mars afflicts 3H of Gemini degree at 3.47" means Mrigsirsh nakstra pada-4. This means Scorpio sign of D9 and its lord is Mars, nakstra lord is also Mars. First house lord of Brain is also Mars.

Gemini sign and 3H with its lord Mercury related to communication, mental equilibrium general relationship and interaction, intelligence, motivation, etc. This is impacted with three dire malefic and its lord Mercury is in acute Paapakartari. The nerve of the native is very weak and distorts the mental equilibrium. Mars is in mrityu bhaga [19-20 Saravali etc.]. Rahu always-retro aspects Mars & Aquarius involve Arudha Lgna, 1HL and 8th lord indicates the problem in brain or neurological disorder of innate or nija dosa, the karmic baggage of past life.

[02] Karka:

Karaka of Brain is Sun and Mars and Sun is aspected by Saturn. Saturn, the karaka of sufferings, afflicts Mercury the karaka of nerves and internal behaviour, perception and communication.

[03] Confirmation in D40

Mars and Sun is debilitated, Mercury retro in acute papakartari. Natal Gemini 3.43 dg means Leo sign in D40 that is posited by Satrun and aspected by Rahu. And if we consider independent aspect of divisional chart then Leo lord Sun is under Rahu, Saturn, Mars aspect and Sun being natural karaka of physique, Brain-head the female is insane and its is mental aberration or bipolar disorder case. This gives us the triplicate confirmation of the sufferings and cursed karma of the previous birth is involved here.

[04] Dasa System:

Since we do not have the proper timing of event, we could not test the dasa part here. Family members did not remember the onset period.

[05] Past Life- cursed Karma

Most Afflicted Nakstra [referred to as MAN hereinafter] is considered as 6H then 8H/L [natal 1H] is the native doing wrongs – sins and 4HL [natal 9H] is prenatal adobe.

The native is in the same manushya yoni [manes world] in the same cast with degraded living. Mars the D9 lord of MAN is with exalted planet and dual sign in both D1 & D9. In addition, Mercury is exalted in D9 but with its natural enemy Martian effect.

8H nakstra from MAN is Utrashada-3 the female and in past life, the native was in her total involvement of selfish, envy activities, and is apathetic towards other. The native was involved in attaining sacred works and renunciation, but due to her selfishness and envies, involved in irreligious and sinful deeds by defaming brethrens and mentor or olden person like father, made them facing penury. Due to this, they cursed her to suffer such the condition and died in sigh. She faced mental disorder and spouseless in this birth. Those who gave support to the native in past life became parents and brothers, are tolerating the native in this birth.

Here Rahu in rasi sandhi and Mars involvement gives the clue of 'Bhtru Shaapa' but Mars in Pushkaramsa is with exalted planet both in D1 & D9 and if we take the same analogy then there are other curses also and is not accurate so I take this ideal method to detect the cursed karma of past life.

[06] General exception

Exception is that Jupiter in Venus sign in 2H aspecting Virgo and Capricorn sign in D1 having nexus to past life indicating chance of total cure if correct remedial measures are taken in time. May be it is require to perform for two three times.

Venus in MAN D9 sign Scorpio having aspect on 7H of Tauraus in D9. Venus is karaka of spouse and 7H and here it owns the same both in D1 & D9. Venus in paapa kartari in both D1 & D9 might have caused delayed or denial marriage. Mercury in paapa kartari in D1 & D9,

Mercury might not support remedial measures, as it is retro.

[07] Expiation

For expiation of this cursed karma, Maharsri Katyayanokta UDAKA SHANTI [ritual performance with water in kalash] should be performed with the help of Vedic Pundit. The native and her parents would be given RUDRA SNANA [bathing with Rudra mantras with the water prepared in those kalashas]. Then give the Daxina [fees of the officiating priest] and do appropriate charities and donations as per the wish and wealth of the native the worshipper. Then pray to dear lords Aaditya [12-Sun], Vasu [eight vasus-beneficent], Rudras [11-Rudra], Vishvedeva [all the Gods or Gods of Pitrus], Marudgana [49- troop of the Maruts] that all my dreadful sins destroyed or removed. Having uttered this prayer often or repeatedly bagging pardon to the Head priest or Head Lord [Brahma-Vishnu-Mahesh], the cursed karma in this manner would become perfectly pure. By doing these rituals, without doubt, the disease would be extinct; the native would get spouse, and children.

Note- For ritual performance of Udaka Shanti do it with the help of highly learned Brahman. There are two schools of this Udaka Shanti, one is Katyayanokta and other is Baudhayanokta, here first envisaged. We do not find any major difference in this and both give the excellent results. It is very important to note that fees and donations-charity is to be done as per one's wish and wealth appropriately nothing compulsory. Charity and donations can be to Brahman, Veda School, Temples, Hospitals, old age home, hostels, Armies etc. etc. It is noteworthy that wish is coupled with one's economic capacity to donate as sometimes we have wish but no money and sometimes we have money but no wish. However, if you have wish to do charity or donation then do not wait, do it by serving needy people, animals, birds, serpents etc. for which no need to have wealth - money. However, do not do it with fear in mind or some expectation but with pious heart and motive, all your cursed karma will be purified. Here Mars, Venus and Mercury are involved so donations or serving hostels, pupil and armies [male & female] is the best expiation.

Chapter – 14

Most Afflicted Anuradha Nakstra

Female – KJL
26-November-1980; 02.00.00 AM; Valsad, India (+05.30 east) 072e54 & 20n37; Ayanamsa 23.34.29.33

Marriage date 29-november-2008 widowed 9-february-2012; Lady faced 'sveta kusta roga' since last many years. She is childless.

D1

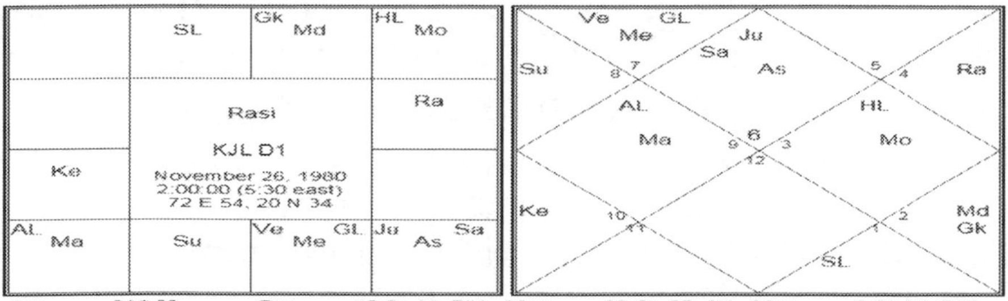

As:	2 Vi 03	**Su:**	10 Sc 11- PiK	**Mo:**	28 Ge 05- AK	**Ma:**	9 Sg 18- GK
Me:	21 Li 54- AmK	**Ju:**	11 Vi 41- MK/Pi	**Ve:**	8 Li 39- DK	**Sa:**	13 Vi 45- BK
Ra:	19 Cn 53	**Ke:**	19 Cp 53	**HL:**	10 Ge 21	**GL:**	26 Li 48

D9

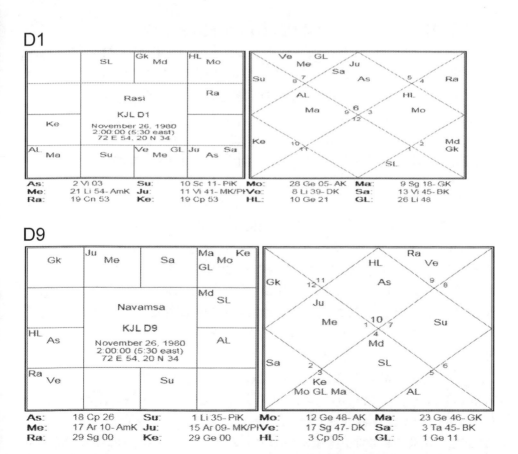

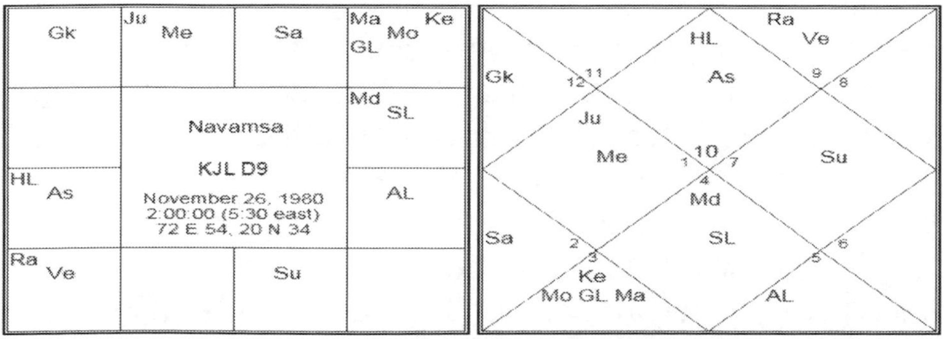

As:	18 Cp 26	**Su:**	1 Li 35- PiK	**Mo:**	12 Ge 48- AK	**Ma:**	23 Ge 46- GK
Me:	17 Ar 10- AmK	**Ju:**	15 Ar 09- MK/Pi	**Ve:**	17 Sg 47- DK	**Sa:**	3 Ta 45- BK
Ra:	29 Sg 00	**Ke:**	29 Ge 00	**HL:**	3 Cp 05	**GL:**	1 Ge 11

D60

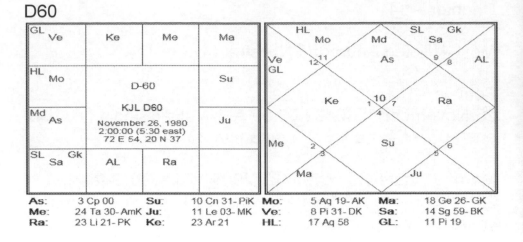

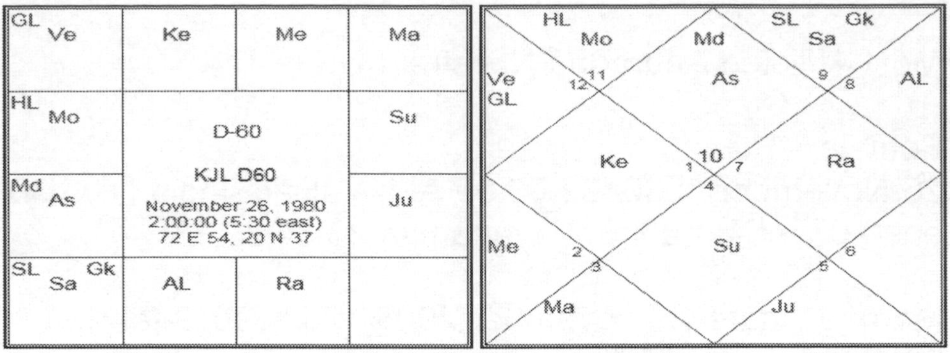

As:	3 Cp 00	**Su:**	10 Cn 31- PiK	**Mo:**	5 Aq 19- AK	**Ma:**	18 Ge 26- GK
Me:	24 Ta 30- AmK	**Ju:**	11 Le 03- MK	**Ve:**	8 Pi 31- DK	**Sa:**	14 Sg 59- BK
Ra:	23 Li 21- PK	**Ke:**	23 Ar 21	**HL:**	17 Aq 58	**GL:**	11 Pi 19

[01] MAN with orbs of 4.00 dg for Rahu:

Taking 4.00 dg orbs of Rahu we find that Scorpio 15.53 dg i.e. Anuradha pada-4 is most afflicted by Rahu [19Cn53 deducing 4.00dg orbs we find Rahu aspect at 15.53dg], Saturn and Sun. Its lord is Saturn, sign lord is Mars, D9 sign is Scorpio, and its lord is Mars. Mars is in acute papa kartari with natal 4H of 'gruhastha ashrama' i.e. home life and 7H of spouse from Moon sign. Mars the karka of death and mishaps lord from Moon. Scorpio sign is 6th from Moon indicates diseased spouse, Mars aspects Moon and Moon sign where Rahu posited; Saturn the 8th lord to Moon sign also aspects [dim] Moon. Again in D9 Moon in Gemini creates the same scenario. So, this is multilateral affliction, indicates wicked and spouse with bad habits of drugs, drinks, smoking etc. Luminaries affliction by dire malefic fingering at white spot and cursed soul and is popularly known as 'PretaShaapa' or 'Pisaacha Pida'. Both are having resemblance to our MAN & its D9 lord.

Mars, Saturn, and Rahu afflict 7H from ascendant. Mars is the lord of 8H of widowhood and Saturn 6H of disease-mishaps-loss of spouse from ascendant. This also confirms the early widowhood. Mars is 64th D9 lord from ascendant. Involvement of 8th lord here points out innate defect or nija dosha. In D9 also Sagittarius is 7H from moon and it is heavily afflicted by nodes and Mars, Jupiter by Rahu.

This bulky affliction gives the clue to widowhood clearly.

[02] Confirmation in Higher Division
15.53 dg Scorpio means Gemini sign of D60, heavily afflicted by three dire malefic Mars, Saturn and Rahu. Also D1 sign Sagittarius where MAN D9 lord posited is also afflicted in D60 by Mars, Gulika & Saturn.

Jupiter in Moon nakstra -Moon in Jupiter nakstra in Kendra to each other forms 'Gajakesri Yoga' in D1, confirmed in D60 should give good results why turned to malice affects. As per BPHS yoga bhanga exists if Moon or Jupiter in relation to combustion or debilitated planet. And when we assess past life karma Yoga cancellation should also be seen with the help of 6th lord [past life karma] and 8th lord [nija dosha]. As per our method we take MAN D9 sing/lord and we find here the Gajakesari Yoga is afflicted. Now good results of this yoga like vibrant, riches, intellect, virtuous and royal favorite are not seen here as it depends on the predominance degree of the yoga. But here the yoga is badly affected if we do not call it cancellation, indication innate defect carried forward from past life. The native faced early widowhood, living in poor condition, facing 'sveta kushta roga' and was doing clerical job on computer. The native was in last birth wise and royal favorite but he has abused her wisdom and betrayed the royal. She abused people, royals also make money out of that and in current birth, and she paid the penalty.

[03] Karaka Element

2H is karaka of spouse as per BPHS and Mercury Venus there with good BAV & SAV points is good to protect the spouse. Even in D9 Sagittarius is having Venus and Jupiter aspect. The only thing is that Venus heavily afflicted in D9 and Mercury in cruel D60 having 8th resemblance from Moon; also as Virgo the sing of 1H of Mercury in mrityu bhaaga [MB]. Sun the Karaka of husband is posited in MAN and debilitated in D9.

[04] Dasa system

Married on 29-November-2008

Widowed on 09-February-2012

Chara Dasa is strongly applicable here in connotation of marriage and widowhood. If we see the marriage yoga on effective date, we have Sagittarius MD and Cancer AD of Chara Dasa; in transit, Jupiter was in Sagittarius sign with 7HL from Venus aspecting Aries and Moon. Mars is our MAN D9 lord. On effective date of widowhood, natal Chara Dasa was Sagittarius MD and Scorpio AD and in transit Scorpio Rahu, aspected by Mars and natal Sagittarius and Mars there is aspected by transit Saturn, posits sign. In natal most afflicted sign is Scorpio.

[05] General Exception

2H is karaka of spouse as per BPHS and Mercury Venus there with good BAV & SAV points is good to protect the spouse. Even in D9 Sagittarius is having Venus and Jupiter aspect.

As we said analogy of cursed karma overpowered 'subha yoga' or exception in the chart. And this yoga or exception may entail good and free cursed karma life if remedial measures taken timely.

[06] Cursed Karma and its expiation

In prenatal adobe the native named Sumitra, was very wise and devotional to people around her. She was highly intellectual & wise, and royal favorite. She abuse royals and make money. She also proved a bad wife for her husband & mother in law too. She took away all their clothes, wealth, and monies deserted her husband and runaway with her friend [8H from MAN D9 lord Mars]. They faced poor living conditions, mother in law afflicted with leprosy and husband in heart wailing pain died after many days, in sigh cursed the native.

Expiation is required for Mars, Moon and Jupiter. Do puruscharana as directed by ritual performance and Vedic astrology regulations. Do appropriate daily japa of MAN ruler Saturn & lord Mitra [Anuradha], charity synonyms to Sun and services according to significations of Sun as per wish and wealth of the native. This may include serve people like father, medications to them, blinds etc. RudraSnana and Vrusostsarga or Preta Bali is suggested here with the help of Vedic Brahmin. By doing this past life sinful deeds of the native will be nullified and native may live comfortable and healthy life.

Chapter-15

Most Afflicted Chitra Nakstra

[01] Female – RtkBht

Date: October 30, 1989; Time: 4:25:00 am; Time Zone: 5:30:00 (East of GMT) Place: 72 E 56' 00", 20 N 38' 00" Valsad, India; Tithi: Sukla Pratipat (Su) (71.84% left);

Nakshatra: Swaati (Ra) (28.63% left) Ayanamsa: 23-41-57.77

Marriage date 18-February-2013; Widowhood 20-November-2013

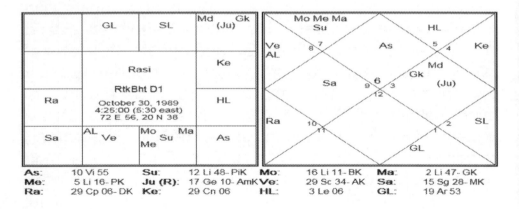

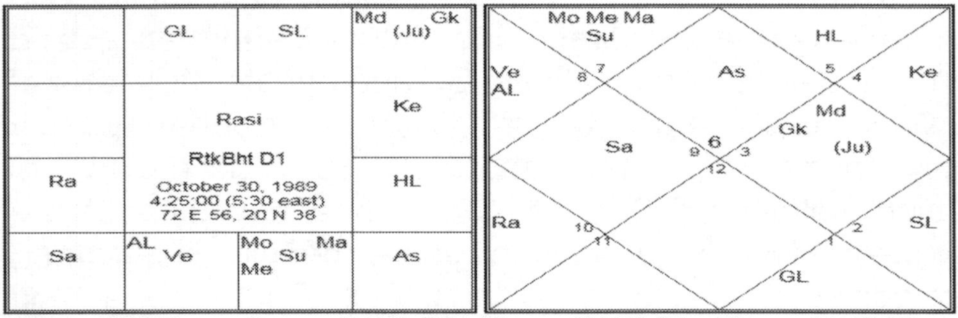

As:	10 Vi 55	**Su:**	12 Li 48- PiK	**Mo:**	16 Li 11- BK	**Ma:**	2 Li 47- GK
Me:	5 Li 16- PK	**Ju (R):**	17 Ge 10- AmK	**Ve:**	29 Sc 34- AK	**Sa:**	15 Sg 28- MK
Ra:	29 Cp 06- DK	**Ke:**	29 Cn 06	**HL:**	3 Le 06	**GL:**	19 Ar 53

D9

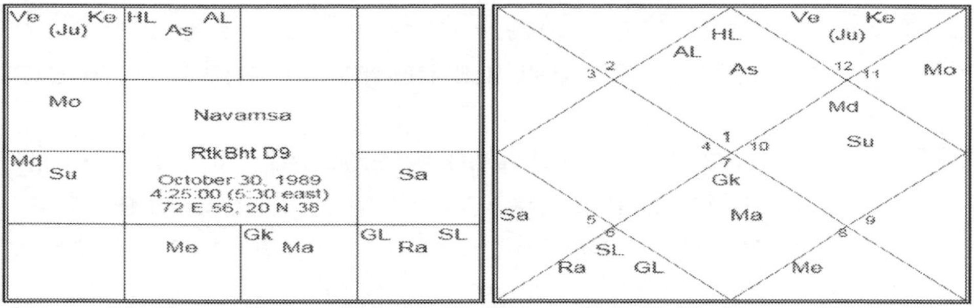

As:	8 Ar 16	**Su:**	25 Cp 14- PiK	**Mo:**	25 Aq 39- BK	**Ma:**	25 Li 04- GK
Me:	17 Sc 25- PK	**Ju (R):**	4 Pi 34- AmK	**Ve:**	26 Pi 09- AK	**Sa:**	19 Le 15- MK
Ra:	21 Vi 51- DK	**Ke:**	21 Pi 51	**HL:**	27 Ar 52	**GL:**	29 Vi 01

D60

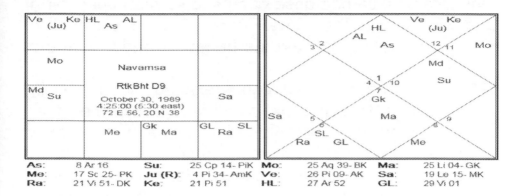

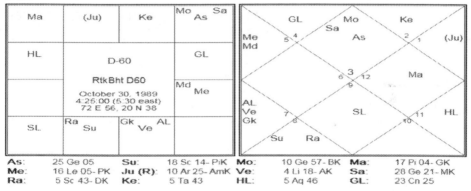

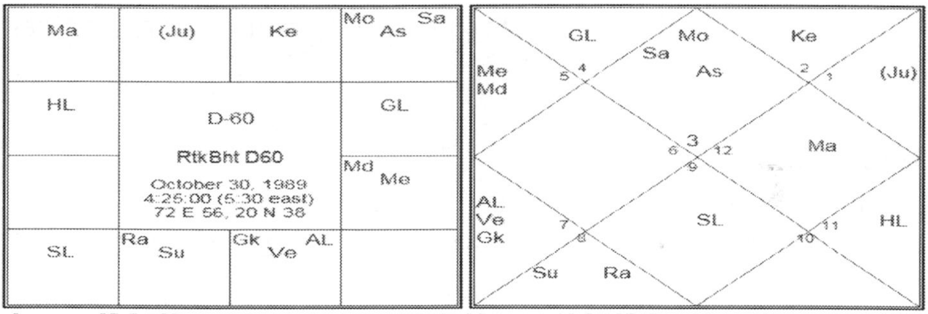

As:	25 Ge 05	**Su:**	18 Sc 14- PiK	**Mo:**	10 Ge 57- BK	**Ma:**	17 Pi 04- GK
Me:	16 Le 05- PK	**Ju (R):**	10 Ar 25- AmK	**Ve:**	4 Li 18- AK	**Sa:**	28 Ge 21- MK
Ra:	5 Sc 43- DK	**Ke:**	5 Ta 43	**HL:**	5 Aq 46	**GL:**	23 Cn 25

[01] MAN with Rahu orbs +3.42 dg and one more afflicting element

Rahu and Mars vitiate Chitra pada-3 at 2.47 dg. Nakstra lord is Mars and D9 lord of this MAN is Venus of Libra sign. Venus is in paapakartari with arudha lagna. Looking to the degree position of luminaries, we find that it is virtual amavasya birth. Venus is in acute Gandata, curel D60 and exchange to Mars. Mars carries A6 [arudha of 6H] in Libra sign of Venus with Moon and Venus is 64th D9 lord from Moon. Involvement of Arudha Lagna, Atmakaraka and A6 into curse planets

indicates soul carried dosa of cursed karma in past birth and will intensify the same. Venus the curse planet in 4H by dg position polluted the home life and fate of the spouse.
MAN D9 sign and its lord Venus exalted with Jupiter in D9 indicates that the native should remember that whatever God do for her is good for future in mysterious miseries. Now see the mystery of widowhood in navamsa chart. See D9 chart independently where Mars and gulika in Libra, the sign 7th to ascendant and 8th to Venus, afflicted by Saturn. This vitiated Mars syndrome in D9 chart made the huge damage to the native.

[02] Karaka
Karaka of 7H, Venus lost its karaka tatva as it is in acute gandanta, cruel D60, and in D9 Saturn, Rahu and Mars in 6-7-8 H which itself is a combination for widowhood. Sun debilitated in D1, inimically postured with Mars and Rahu aspect in D9. 2nd the house of karaka of spouse with Mars syndrome with amavasya luminaries and sign lord Venus is helpless in bala avastha as said.

[03] Confirmation in Higher Division
Chitra pada -3 of Libra sign at 2.47 dg means D60 Pisces sign heavily afflicted by Mars, Rahu and Saturn so the MAN D9 and its lord Mars. Venus the si lord of MAN posited in Libra with Mars aspect in D60.

This mars syndrome is confirm wrt Libra and Venus our concerned sign and lord. This celestially triggered in Kala Chakra Dasa [hereinafter referred to as KCD].

[04] Dasa system
See at the effective date of Marriage [18-Feb-2013] the natal KCD Taurus MD_Libra AD lord Venus, from there 7H of marriage is Taurs and transit Jupiter from Taurus dimly aspects Venus help fructify the marriage. At the time of death of spouse on 20-November-2014, the MD Taurus sign and lord Venus and AD sign Scorpio and lord Mars are having afflicted in natal, in transit Saturn-Rahu in 2/12 & 6/8 yoga.

For the readers' reference, I am giving the shloka from BPHS [Mumbai Khemraj edition] for spouse death timing.

कलत्रकारकः खेटस्तदा स्त्रीराशिचिन्तनं॥ तत्त्रिकोणदशायां च कलत्र निधनं भवेत्॥ ३१॥

एवं भावकलत्रादितद्दशारुढयन्त्रके॥ चिन्तयेदायुः सामर्थ्यंसर्वं फ़लसमानकं॥३३॥... अ-

२३॥

kalatrakārakaḥ kheṭastadā strīrāśicintanaṁ || tattrikoṇadaśāyāṁ ca kalatra nidhanaṁ bhavet|| 31|| evaṁ bhāvakalatrāditaddaśāruḍhayantrake || cintayedāyuḥ sāmarthyaṁsarvaṁ falasamānakaṁ ||33|| ... a|23||

First determined the karaka [promising marriage] and think of spouse sign from there, and dasa of trine sign from that spouse sign will cause death of spouse. In the same manner from respective bhava like kaltra [spouse], the dasa mechanism of that karaka or its trine may cause death. From the ascendant or karaka [means arudha of that house i.e. 7H, or kaltra bhava itself] house first of all assess longevity efficacy of the bhava then judiciously see the results and death.

The verse is applicable here and I would evaluate the same wrt charts of widowhood in next part if blessings of Sages & God allow me to do so.

[05] General exception
Exception is Jupiter as 7th lord in Kendra should resist the odd but failed to do so as itself afflicted by Mandi and Saturn. In D9 also affliction stands the way of soothing and there is no exception or overriding rule available.

[06] Cursed Karma and its expiation
The native was in Manes world in India near pious river Yamuna town of Hastipura. [Venus MAN D9 lord is exalted in D9]. Her name was Bhomira [4H from MAN Ushada-2 – alphabet 'BHO']. Bhomari was a devotee of lord Shiva &Parvati and do many vratas. She was beautiful looking, living with all her family including brother of her grandfather. However, she misbehaves with them but loves them and they love her very much and overlook her behaviour and attitude. She married to a good-natured rich spouse, living with his family. The spouse gave her free hand over his riches. The brother of her spouse was a wise man and the royal favourite. After marriage she planned conspiracy made spouse death and lives with the brother with riches of her late spouse. Unfortunately the brother of spouse also died. She returned to her natal house living with her family again. There she underwent austerities and do penance [व्रत तप ... vrata tapa] and made her pious. The family members gave her cooperation and overlook her conspiracy, became parents in this current birth era.

Due to this sin, she was cursed and faced early widowhood and bequeathed the death claim of around Rs.16.00 lacks.

[07] Expiation
She would overcome the blemish of this cursed karma when do penance of Arundhati ... चैत्र शुक्ल तृतीया अरुन्धति व्रत... caitra śukla tṛtīyā arundhati vrata. Here japa, self-study [soul thinking of vrata story i.e. vrata katha], charities, sacrifices and expiation all is included in this vrata.

Shankha Yoga [JP-Subramanyam Sashtri CH-7 V138/139] is formed when ascendant lord and 10HL are in moveable sign and 9HL is strong. Here, Venus the 9HL in exchange to Mars and in D9 exalted with suffice shadbala is strong and Mercury as 1H & 10H lords in moveable sign Libra.

The result of the yoga is that the native has a lots of enjoyment, be compassionate, blessed with spouse, wealth and lands, engaged in practice of virtue, will possess the sacred scripture, will be well-conducted, beneficent, and may live beyond 81 yrs. The yoga is afflicted, being Venus in acute gandanta and is vitiated as said hereinabove.

Due to vrata and tapa the native virtually enjoying all good results of the yoga and due to her bad karma she faced early widowhood.
Now to rectify do vrata and appropriated donations-charity etc. is one view. Another view is to rectify the

karma such as appropriated to this yoga results. Use wealth and lands in donations to needy people, engaged oneself in virtuous life and be compassionate, are some karma native should follow.

There are two views for interpreting the yoga results wrt past life karma. For good karma, the yoga formed and native, get the result of the yoga and due to sinful karma the yoga cancelled or vitiated and the native suffered a lot. Veda School says that karma can be rectified by karma only, and whenever sinful karma does by native, the yoga will be cancelled or vitiated and it can be rectified by good karma. Kalpashastra school says that expiation-remedial measures will help the native enjoy the fruits of the yoga and yoga cancelled or vitiated due to bad karma of prenatal adobe one may do Japa, Havana, appropriate donations and charity to rectify that.

[02] Male: HBt
Date: October 5, 1961; Time: 12:05:00 PM; Time Zone: 5:30:00 (East of GMT); Place: 72 E 56' 00", 20 N 38' 00" Valsad, India; Tithi: Krishna Ekadasi (Ma) (14.42% left)
Ayanamsa: 21-52-36.82 [Raman]

D1

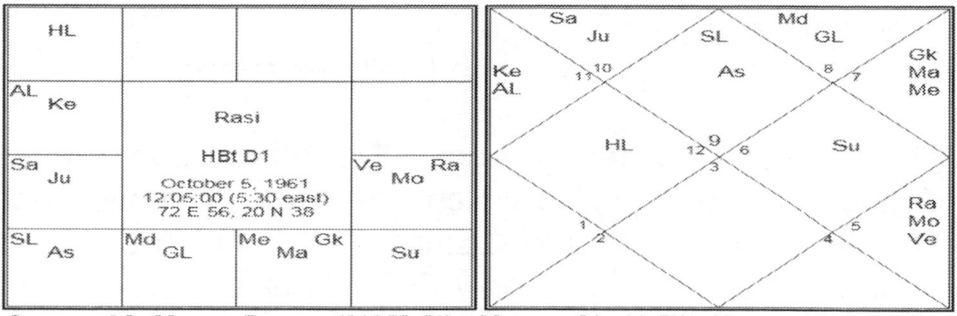

As:	4 Sg 28	**Su**:	19 Vi 55- BK	**Mo**:	0 Le 11- DK	**Ma**:	10 Li 28- PiK
Me:	14 Li 26- MK	**Ju**:	5 Cp 40- PK	**Ve**:	22 Le 19- AmK	**Sa**:	1 Cp 25- GK
Ra:	4 Le 36- AK	**Ke**:	4 Aq 36	**HL**:	5 Pi 18	**GL**:	13 Sc 42

D9

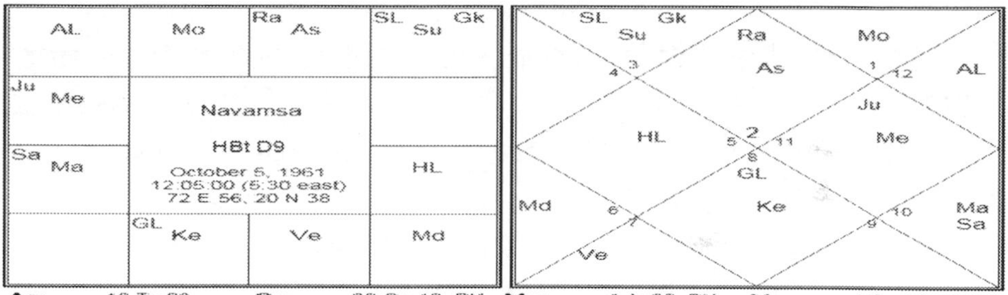

As:	10 Ta 08	**Su**:	29 Ge 13- BK	**Mo**:	1 Ar 39- DK	**Ma**:	4 Cp 12- PiK
Me:	9 Aq 54- MK	**Ju**:	20 Aq 59- PK	**Ve**:	20 Li 47- AmK	**Sa**:	12 Cp 41- GK
Ra:	11 Ta 21- AK	**Ke**:	11 Sc 21	**HL**:	17 Le 39	**GL**:	3 Sc 22

D40

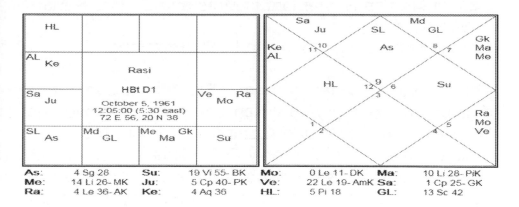

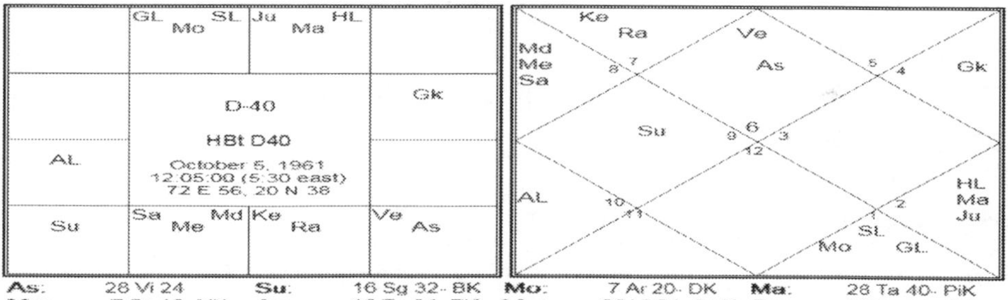

As:	28 Vi 24	**Su**:	16 Sg 32- BK	**Mo**:	7 Ar 20- DK	**Ma**:	28 Ta 40- PiK
Me:	7 Sc 18- MK	**Ju**:	16 Ta 34- PK	**Ve**:	22 Vi 24- AmK	**Sa**:	26 Sc 21- GK
Ra:	3 Li 46- AK	**Ke**:	3 Li 46	**HL**:	1 Ta 48	**GL**:	8 Ar 18

[01] MAN with orbs and one more element of affliction

Taking 5dg orbs of Mars and 4dg+ for Saturn we find most afflicted Chitra-4 naksra at 5.28 dg Libra and its

sign lord is Venus, star lord is Mars and D9 lord is Mars of Scorpio sign.
Mars is with Gulika and in curel D60 'Heramba'.

The native is suffering from PUJ obstruction, urine drainage disease due to which one-kidney removed on 2/3-May-1997, other one repaired on 3-July-1997, and drainage made, working only 60%. This is birth defect. In 2013-2014, the same problem reoccurred and same surgery of drainage made on 5-February-2014 now single kidney works at 30/35 % only.

Please see that Libra is the sign indicating kidney and Mars our MAN D9 lord there with Saturn aspect damaging with Chitra nakstra rules the same [according to some astrologers]. Venus also received aspect of Saturn in D9. Mars 7th and 12th from its sign doing the damage particularly in this area as Moon the urine drainage karaka and Venus the lord of Libra is with Rahu. Gemini 8th from our MAN D9 sign also contributes the same as its lord is in Libra with Mars. 7H Gemini sign represents Kidney here. Libra at 4.27 dg [bhava madya] in Mrityu Bhaga [Saravali etc 19-20] is also causing the damage.

[02] Karaka [Causative]
Karaka of Kidney is Venus, Moon for urine drainage and Mercury the urine drainage tube. Moon is in acute gandata with no exception. We have seen that these elements are duly spoiled. The same is confirmed in D40.

[03] Higher Division [D40]

Scorpio sign and lord Mars is afflicted in Scorpio-Taurus axis with Mandi and Jupiter - Mercury in discomfort zone. 5.28 dg of Libra means Scorpio sign in D40. Libra lord Venus debilitated.

[04] Dasa System [please note that we have taken Raman Ayanamsa]
KCD is Taurus MD _ Libra AD on May3, 1997and Libra is duly afflicted in natal and from natal Libra, transit Saturn-ketu 6th to it and from natal Venus it is in 8th . Transit Mars is with natal Venus-Chandra. Vimsottari Dasa is Moon MD _ Rahu AD. From natal Moon-Rahu transit, Saturn-Ketu is 8th to it and Mars is with them.

On February 05, 2014, Vimsottari Dasa is Rahu _ Rahu, in natal Rahu is inimically poised damaging karakas Moon & Venus. Venus is the lord of 8th to Libra where MAN D9 lord Mars is posited. In transit Saturn is aspecting natal Rahu-Moon. KCD is Gemini MD _ Aries AD and natal sign/lord are afflicted and in transit Gemini is apspected by Rahu Aries posited by Ketu. 53rd yr running means SCD year is Aries sign and is applicable here.

[05] Exception
There is good exception in the chart. Wealth lord and ascendant lord conjunct in 2H and Sun-Venus-Mercury in Shrunkhla Yoga gives the economic power and inherent strength to the native to fight against all odds and adversities. The native is living with 30/35 % of single kidney working.

[06] Past life cursed karma & Expiation

Here we will not envisage prenatal adobe place and name etc but try to evaluate the cursed karma
The native was highly acclaimed scholar pundit and well known for his knowledge and intellect. He had many enemies but he ruled over them. [Taurus sign natal 6H, being 8th to MAN D9 lord Mars having Jupiter aspect]. He has having Ashrama with all kind of intellectual and commercial activity and many disciples were working there [Gemini sign 8th from D9 sign Scorpio and natal 7H]. He was married and having children. He was attracted to one beautiful looking disciple woman in early 40's and run away with her. They live in remote place. He then realised his mistake and stoic condition surrounded him. He started intoxication, faced penury, and could not look after the woman. They starved for many days and died. Due to this sinful karma, the native was detected with the dreadful disease in late 40's in current birth era.

Expiation
In right manner hear [do soul thinking] 'Kurma Purana', does 'Radra Patha' and worship auspicious Devtas. It should be done in accordance with custom rule to destroy all the sins. Do sacrifice in the regular four-cornered 'havana kunda'. Feed needy/ starving couples. For its appeasing suitable-proper charity-donations-devotional, service to class of people or live being is to be done. By doing, this without doubt physical well-being is gained or minimized.

Note – Kurma Purana is suggested here to purify one's self. Here there are Isvar Gita and Vyasa Gita.

Mahakali 1008 names is worshipped and many more for expiation.

Chapter- 16

Most Afflicted Pushya Nakstra

Female-RgniBthMss

Date: September 19, 1971; Time: 21:45:00 pm; Time Zone: 5:30:00 (East of GMT) Place: 76 E 42' 00", 11 N 24' 00" ; Ooty, India ; Tithi: Sukla Pratipat (Su) (97.73% left); Nakshatra: Uttara Phalguni (Su) (53.30% left); Ayanamsa: 23-26-47.80

D1

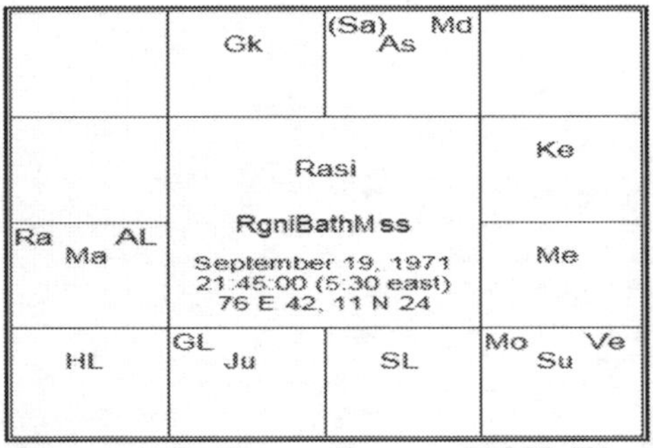

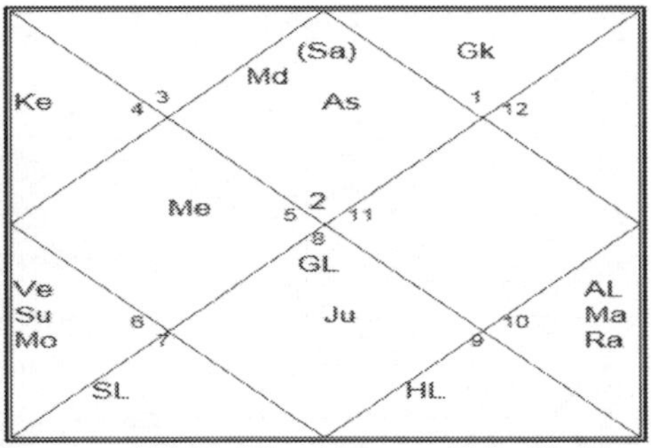

As:	1 Ta 15	Su:	2 Vi 37- DK	Mo:	2 Vi 54- GK	Ma:	19 Cp 07- AK
Me:	17 Le 31- AmK	Ju:	7 Sc 41- PK	Ve:	8 Vi 50- PiK	Sa (R):	13 Ta 05- BK
Ra:	20 Cp 30- MK	Ke:	20 Cn 30	HL:	16 Sg 33	GL:	23 Sc 24

D9

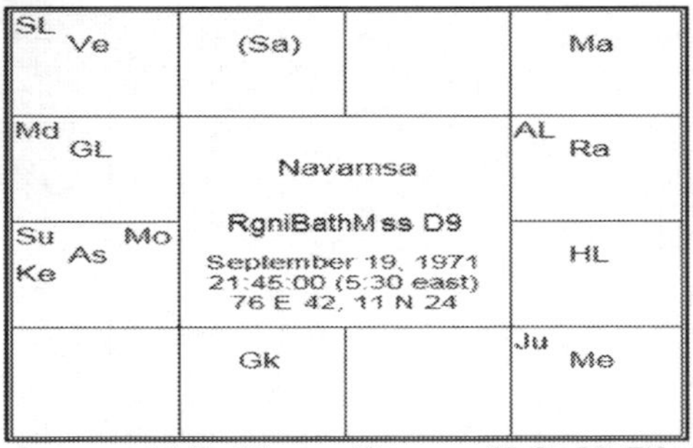

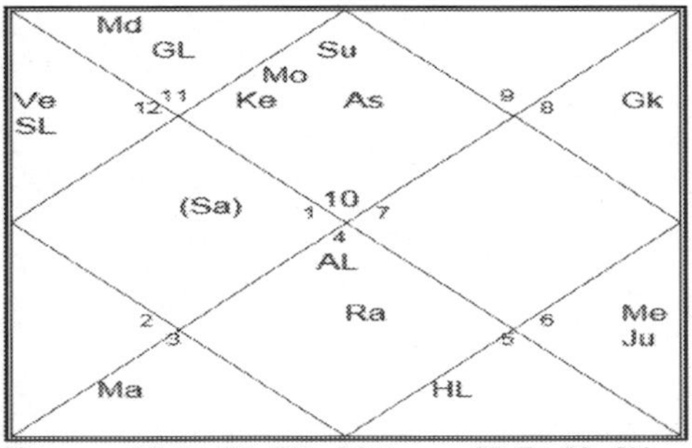

As:	11 Cp 14	Su:	23 Cp 36- DK	Mo:	26 Cp 03- GK	Ma:	22 Ge 03- AK
Me:	7 Vi 35- AmK	Ju:	9 Vi 06- PK	Ve:	19 Pi 30- PiK	Sa (R):	27 Ar 42- BK
Ra:	4 Cn 28- MK	Ke:	4 Cp 28	HL:	29 Le 00	GL:	0 Aq 35

D45

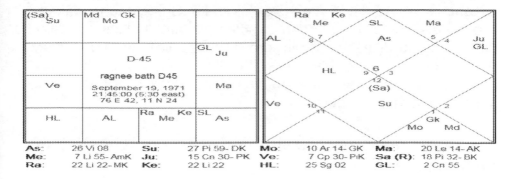

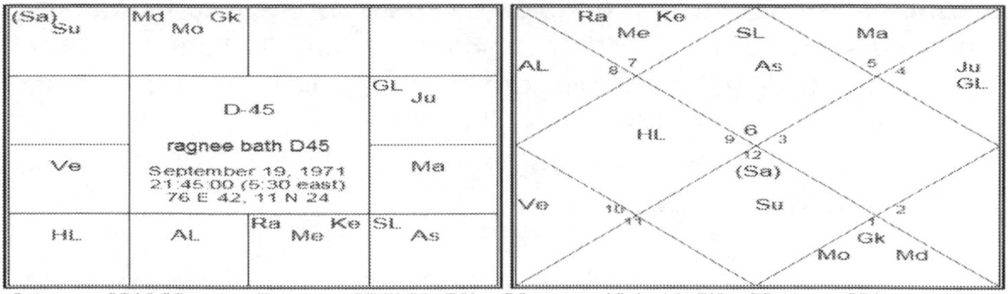

As:	26 Vi 08	**Su:**	27 Pi 59- DK	**Mo:**	10 Ar 14- GK	**Ma:**	20 Le 14- AK
Me:	7 Li 55- AmK	**Ju:**	15 Cn 30- PK	**Ve:**	7 Cp 30- PiK	**Sa (R):**	18 Pi 32- BK
Ra:	22 Li 22- MK	**Ke:**	22 Li 22	**HL:**	25 Sg 02	**GL:**	2 Cn 55

''------- I am reproducing the mail of the native without name
-Dear punditji,
I was born in xxx near xxx if that makes a difference.
Rest all birth details are accurate.
Present condition is another relapse [of multiple sclerosis: two new lesions one in spine and one in brain. As yet i am not in hospital but may have to in the next few days.
I am told that th saad satti is coming to an end this month and the presence of mangal is making me sick. Pl confirm.
I don't understand how my routine or arrangements has any bearing on my chart but i try and do everything myself. I used to work from home but now for one year I no longer work and still getting through th day is difficult.
Pl advise.
Regards,
xxxxxxx
Previous - Diagnosis on 11.10.2006; 2nd attack early Feb 2009; 3rd attack September 2009; 4th attack march April 2012 and latest in December 2012.
Pl let me know what th results of this research are and if there is an astrological treatment.
''-------

Multiple sclerosis- A chronic, typically progressive disease involving damage to the sheaths of nerve cells in the brain and spinal cord, whose symptoms may include numbness, impairment of speech and of muscular coordination, blurred vision, and severe fatigue, also known as disseminated sclerosis. Multiple sclerosis affects the brain and spine and your entire nervous system is impacted and muscles are compressed or fibrosis and becomes useless; the person has to do everything with either support or in the bed – wheelchair.

Diagnosis – 3-7-11 H, Leo sign, karaka Sun, Magha nakstra represents spinal cord, Pushya sclerosis are in joint if malice caused spine disease. Brain lord & causatives are 1HL, Mars, Aries sign, Sun and Mercury with 3H, Gemini sign the most important for the sheaths of nerves cells. Karaka of Muscles is Mars, Moon the dehadhipati.

[01] Most afflicted Nakstra [orbs taken is 4.00-5.00 degree for all planets]

Nodes at 20.29.49 dg and taking orbs at 5.00 dg we find that Cancer degree at 15.29.49 is the most afflicted by nodes, Saturn [13Ta04] and Mars [19Cp06]. Star most afflicted is Pushya-4.

Sign lord is Moon; Nakstra lord of Pushya is Saturn; and D9 lord of this afflicted nakstra is [5th navamsa of Cancer] Mars of Scorpio sign.

Scorpio sign is important here and it posited by Jupiter lord of chronic disease the 8H aspected by Saturn retro. Jupiter lacking shadabala [75% only], Cancer-Scorpio-Pisces sign represent Spine here. From Sun-Moon ascendant, is also sanely applicable.

3rd house is the house of locomotive for the entire body, rules the nerves system & spine beginning which is severely damage by nodes and Saturn-Mars caused in multiple sclerosis of spine. 3HL [MAN sign lord] Moon paxbalahina, karaka Sun is in cruel D60 so also nakstra lord Saturn. 1H posited by retro Saturn-Mandi and Sun paxabal hina with debilitated planet Venus the lord of disease & physique, dimly aspected by MB planet Rahu in 5H, which affect 11H also by aspect.

[02] Another element of affliction

Rahu is in mrityu bhaga, Mars is the lord 64th D9 from ascendant and Moon. Degree position of Sun-Moon shows the virtual birth is in amavasya tithi and ascendant lord debilitated. Involvement of arudhapada [Capricorn sign, Mars-Rahu] and 8HL indicated innate or inborn defect and related to nija dosha. Jupiter is missing Shadbala. Avastha of Moon is Mrita, Svapna, Lajjit and Kopita, Jupiter is Vriddha, Svapana, and Khala could not protect the native. The sign lord of Pushya Moon is paxabala hina [looking to the degree positions it is amavasya birth].

[03] Confirmation in higher division
Cancer sign at 15.29.49 dg is the most afflicted AMSA in the chart and this means Pisces sign in D45 and wildly afflicted by Saturn-Sun-Mars and Jupiter aspects all spine signs here, means remedial measures would work and the native fight against all the odds. Saturn, karaka of sclerosis is nakstra lord and Mars, karaka of muscles & brain is D9 lord of Pushya-4. Mercury the kraka of locomotion and nerves system is afflicted by the nodes so the Moon karaka of 'deha' with Mandi/Gulika in D45.

[04] Karaka
Karaka and lords of brain, spine and nerves are discussed in the beginning. Mercury is afflicted by Mars

and also Magha naksta whose lord Ketu is heavily afflicted in 3H. We see that the other karaka elements are heavily afflicted to cause the disease.

[05] Dasa system, its affliction in natal and transit
Diagnosis on 11.10.2006; 2nd attack early Feb 2009; 3rd attack September 2009; 4th attack march April 2012 and latest in December 2012.
11-October-2006
Vimsottari Dasa:
Rah MD: 1991-11-30 (11:32:29) - 2009-11-30 (2:16:21)
Sun AD: 2006-06-17 (6:17:36) - 2007-05-11 (0:17:48)
Pratyantardasas in this AD:
Rah: 2006-08-21 (5:37:25) - 2006-10-10 (2:28:51)

The MD lord Rahu is in MB and afflicted by Mars.
AD lord Sun in Virgo paxabal hina in cruel D60 aspected by Rahu in natal and in transit heavily afflicted by Saturn from Cancer, Mars in Virgo and Rahu in Pisces [very dim].
This caused the disease and PD lord is Rahu supports the view and very important is the next PD lord is Jupiter and the native was then fighting against the onset of the ailment.
Just before the attack, a solar eclipse was on 22-sept-2006 though not visible in India its planetary impact is visible as explained.

Februaru-2009
Vimsottari Dasa:
Rah MD: 1991-11-30 - 2009-11-30
Mars AD: 2008-11-12 - 2009-11-30
Pratyantardasas in this AD:

Jup: 2009-01-28 - 2009-03-19

Again Rahu MD and AD lord is Mars and PD lord Jupiter and the same episode continued. See the transit effect also and onset of 'sani Sade sati'.

March-April – 2012
Vimsottari Dasa:
Jup MD: 2009-11-30 (2:16:21) - 2025-11-30 (4:39:17)
Sat AD: 2012-01-16 (18:49:33) - 2014-07-31 (7:53:47)
Pratyantardasas in this AD:
Sat: 2012-01-16 (18:49:33) - 2012-06-10 (22:40:55)

The MD – AD lords are duly afflicted in the natal and also see the transit you will find that both are afflicted by nodes and Jupiter is by Saturn [in 12th to it] and Mars. Looking to the transit and natal Jupiter may not much helpful now, fighting the MSS.

[06] Exception
General exception is Jupiter and Venus influence on 7H & 11H, Mars exalted both in D1 & D9. The native was fighting the odds at initial stages but could not resist the relapses and severly affected. This is because, Jupiter missing Shadbal the basic strength and Vimsopaka Bala the dasa strength. Venus is debilitated in D1 and D9 [due to Jupiter position in Virgo]. Jupiter in Kendra and Venus in trikona is a divine bless.

[07] Cursed Karma in prenatal adobe
The native was in previous birth Bihar land and was a gardener [florist], and her name was Roma. She was poor and devoted to worship of Lord Shri Vishnu all the

time. She was devoted to her husband. Once the dearest friend [सुहृद ... suhrada = dearest friend, friend near to heart] of her grandpa came to her house, seeing [her] poor condition, the rich man felt grieved. With the florist, dearest friend of grandpa came to his own house. She devoted to the friend of grandpa and daily sells flowers and garland. One day the dearest friend was afflicted with dreadful disease in body. The florist at that time gave up the devotional service to this friend and lives happily. She [the florist] with her spouse help took away all the wealth, house and outhouse or his family life. The bed-ridden old friend constantly got the severe pain and sorrow. At the time of death the old friend was in bedridden condition, gave the dreadful and acute curse to her and died. Then after many days she with her spouse died and were truly fell in the hell and then after various births got the manes female body to suffer in current era. The karma brought from previous birth inclined to produce disease in body due to crooked [cruel] sins and her spouse of previous birth also became the spouse of this birth.

[08] Expiation

In right manner hear [do soul thinking] 'Shiva Purana', does 'Chandi Patha' japa and worship auspicious Devtas. It should be done in accordance with custom rule to destroy all the sins. Do sacrifice in the regular four cornered 'havana kunda'. For its appeasing suitable-proper charity-donations-devotional service to class of people or live being is to be done. By doing this without doubt physical well being is gained or minimized.

Note- Here it is noteworthy that devotional services to class of people is envisaged by the scribe as it will be the most suitable and proper karma to do. The logic is that you have done wrong now you do expiation for that and do the good to others as we did not remember what we do in the previous birth and this is the most easy way to ward off you cursed karma and with this to do japa homa is to take the ultimate serenity of god.

Yoga cancelled or vitiated here is Matsya Yoga [JP-Subramanyam Sashtri CH-7 V146/147]. 9H occupied by malefic Rahu-Mars, 5H is occupied by mixed planet Venus-Sun/Moon, 4h or 8H occupied by Malefic and here Mercury is aspected by Mars and is in paapa kartari having Sun sign influence. But the yoga is cancelled when we see degree position i.e. chalit chart. The results are that the native is very compassionate, have virtues, intelligence strength etc. However, the woman did not adhere to this in past life and the result is reverse. The native did sinful karma in past life and is suffering in the current era. She should do expiation and should adhere to the results like compassionate, virtues, take religious merit etc.

Chapter- 17

Most Afflicted Magha Nakstra

[01] Female- RidiPDsi
Date: September 18, 1985; Time: 11:56:00 am; Time Zone: 5:30:00 (East of GMT); Place: 72 E 56' 00", 20 N 38' 00" Valsad, India; Ayanamsa: 22-12-41.25 [Raman]

```
               Rasi      D1
+-----------------------------------+
|\              / \    Ke        /|
| \    9       /     \   Mo     /  |
|   \        /         \    7   /  |
|     \    /    Sa       \   /    |
|       \ /                \ /     |
|JuR    x Gk    As        x    Su  |
| 10   /  \               / \ 6    |
|     /     \    Md    /      \    |
|   /        \        /         \  |
|  /           \  8  /  Me        \ |
|/   11         \ /              \|
|                x    Ma          |
|\              / \      5      /|
| \            /     \ Ve      /  |
|   \        /         \      /   |
|     \    /            \    /    |
|       \ /               \ /     |
|12     x      AL         x    4   |
|       / \               / \      |
|     /     \    2      /     \    |
|   /        \        /         \  |
|  /   Ra     \     /       3    \ |
|/  1           \ /              \|
+-----------------------------------+
```

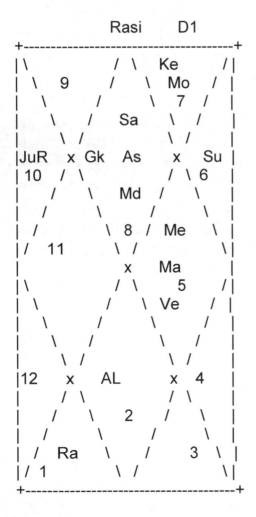

Planetary details are as under.

Body	Longitude	Nakshatra	Pada	Rasi	Navamsa	D60
Lagna	17 Sc 18' 53.26"	Jey	1	8	9	6
Sun – GK	3 Vi 05' 05.20"	Upha	2	6	10	12
Moon – AmK	20 Li 44' 12.54"	Vis	1	7	1	12
Mars – MK	13 Le 00' 02.06"	Magha	4	5	4	7
Mercury – AK	29 Le 07' 40.03"	Uph	1	5	9	3
Jupiter(R)- BK	15Cp 16' 56.20"	Sravana	2	10	2	4
Venus - PK	3 Le 07' 25.25	Magha	1	5	1	11
Saturn – DK	1 Sc 33' 06.97"	Visa	4	8	4	11
Rahu – PiK	17 Ar 45' 55.48	Bhar	2	1	6	12
Ketu	17 Li 45' 55.48"	Swa	4	7	12	6
Maandi	15 Sc 19' 09.96"	Anu	4	8	8	2
Gulika	5 Sc 17' 10.84"	Anu	1	8	5	6
MAN12.45 dg	12 Leo 45	Magha	4	5	4	6

The lady married on 01-July-2007 and widowed on 11-April-2009; Husband died in car accident in London. She bequeathed rupees eighty lacks of death claim for this accidental death.

[01] MAN with orbs, one more element of affliction and Karaka element

Taking Rahu orbs at -5.00 dg we find that Leo 12.45 dg i.e. Magha-4 is most afflicted by Rahu, Mars and dimly by Saturn. In Leo Mercury in Rasi Sandhi and Venus in debilitated sign due to Sun in Virgo posit the sign. Mercury the utmost Maraka owning 8H & 11H afflict MAN sign lord Sun, karaka of husband. MAN D9 sign is Cancer and lord Moon, nakstra lord is Ketu. 7H from Moon is Aries lord Mars. Moon is in cruel D60, Vaidhriti Yoga, Visti Karana and 64th D9 lord from herself, which is inauspicious with nodal affliction in 12th house of final exit as malefic. In D9 Saturn- Mars afflict our MAN D9 sign in 8H of widowhood; there Moon-Venus is aspected by Saturn. Magha-4 is nakstra most afflicted and its lord is Ketu. 7HL Venus heavily afflicted and its Libra sign [the natural zodiac sign of marriage] posited by Moon-Ketu our MAN D9 lord. MAN D9 sing is the 3H sign from natal 7H of premature death of marriage. From our MAN D9 lord Moon, Aries is 7H, its lord Mars is afflicted by Saturn and Rahu in our MAN. These are the root cause of widowhood.

As per hora shastra 2H, 7H and their lords with kaltra karka & Ascendant if afflicted caused loss and or separation of spouse. Here 7H, 7HL and karamak of spouse Venus afflicted by Satrun [6HL of mishaps to Venus the 7HL] -Mars [12HL of loss of spouse to 7H] - Rahu in our MA nakstra Magha, Venus debilitated or inimically posed in cruel D60. Saturn and Gulika/Mandi posit Ascendnat. 2HL in our MAN D9 lord Moon naktra debilitated aspected by Saturn. Accident is also seen from 3H from spouse i.e. 9H lord Moon our MAN D9 lord Moon in 12H i.e. 6H to spouse with ketu indicates accident in foreign land [Mangal vart vartate ketu in 6H from 7H] while in conveyance [3H from 7H]. This yoga of loss of spouse is applicable here. Ascendant carries arudha of 7H indicating soul carrying the burden of past life karma towards spouse. Venus Karak is in Bala avastha, Deena, Susupta and khal avastha. In D9 Venus is with our MAN D9 lord aspected by Saturn. Saturn in D9 afflicts 7HL from Moon, our MAN D9 sign and Venus. Venus-Moon affliction in toto indicates love marriage with pathetic end of marriage.

[02] Higher Division

Leo 12.45 dg means Virgo D60 posited by Ketu-Gulika in relation to our MAN D9 lord Moon-Rahu-Sun in 1/7

House axis. D9 sign of MAN is posited by retro Jupiter aspected by Rahu from its sign Pisces and indicates sudden event in foreign land.

[03] Dasa System [I have taken birthplace for dasa & transit and one may take accident place London also for research purpose]

The lady married on 01-July-2007 and widowed on 11-April-2009

Kalachakra Dasa (From Moon of D-1, Apasavya, Paramayush: 86 yr, Deha: Cn, Jiva: Sg):
Ta (Anu3) MD: 2001-09-14 (23:12:06) - 2017-09-15 (1:40:58)
Li (Rohi2) AD: 2006-05-27 (19:41:06) - 2009-06-01 (0:06:33)

The marriage event date does not confirm the powerful marriage yoga for the woman and on the contrary, it is malice in transit and dasa.
On the spouse death date please see the transit position of Mars-Rahu-Saturn and picture is clear for the heart-wailing trauma.

On 11-April-2009
Transit Saturn – aspect natal Libra where our MAN Moon-Ketu posited
Transit Ketu – In natal Cancer sign
Transit Rahu – Aspects natal Sun, the sign lord of our MAN and 6th to Leo
Transit Mars – Aspects natal Sun

[04] Exception
Visti karana is exception here and there is no afflicting element on this accord. Jupiter aspects Sun, Jupiter, Mercury, Saturn and Ketu are in Pushkar amsha!!!! Does this help the native bequeathing the death claim of Rs.80/- Lacks the soothing for the heart wailing trauma!!

[05] Past life cursed karma & its expiation
The native was famous and virtuous daughter of a Brahman. She did many Vrata and Tapa before marriage. She married to an ascetic and self-existent Brahman. Her husband was a famous having own Ashrama, his name was Vaamana. Vaamana love her very much and care for her. The native inclined to sex with a handsome disciple of the Ashrama of his husband. The ascetic husband came to know this and was suffered heart wailing pain. He cursed the native and vacated her from his life and Ashrama. Father opposes the native and do not wish to keep her, but mother was in love sooth the native, father in love of daughter at last keep her, and overlooked her sin. Due to this cursed karma, the native faced early widowhood. Parents who kept her also in this current era are parents of the native. Due to her Tapa and Vrata she belongs to good well-to-do Brahman family in current era and bequeathed the death claim monies.

For expiation of cursed karma of the native, do ritual pooja of carved idol of LaxmiNarayana and by its side male figure on gold or silver or panchadhaatu leaf/card; carved Shapa Nashna mantra also. Do puruscharna of Sarveshvar Bhagvaan Papa Shamana mantra. Do appropriate donation and devotional service to needy couple or donate on marriage ceremony of needy couple.

Pasa Yoga [JP-Subramanyam Sashtri CH-7 V173/179 results] formed as all planets are in four signs or house [nodes not considered], being nodes not considered.
The yoga results are the native is very clever in the acquisition of wealth and virtues, will talkative and have sons. Due to past life karma the yoga is broken by Venus vitiated in magha nakstra and the native faced widowhood and bequeathed the wealth.

[02] Male-PrtkPndya

Date:June 16, 1978; Time: 23:33:00 pm; Time Zone: 5:30:00 (East of GMT); Place: 72 E 57' 00", 20 N 45' 00" Bilimora, India
Vyatipata yoga; Ayanamsa: 22-06-36.35

Body	Longitude	Star	Pada	D1	D9	D40
Ascendnat	7 Aq 44' 32.83"	Satatarka	1	11	9	11
Sun	1 Ge 12' 36.86"	Mrigshira	3	3	7	2
Moon	10 Vi 36' 54.01"	Hast	1	6	1	9
Mars	8 Le 14' 50.73"	Magha	3	5	3	11
Mercury	1 Ge 32' 37.12"	Mrigshira	3	3	7	3
Jupiter	19Ge58' 54.20"	Ardra	4	3	12	3
Venus	6 Cn 06' 57.42"	Pushya	1	4	5	3
Saturn	3 Le 39' 57.76"	Magha	2	5	2	5
Rahu	10 Vi 02' 30.55"	Hasta	1	6	1	8
Ketu	10 Pi 02' 30.55	U Bhadra	3	12	7	8
Mandi	0 Ta 52' 33.96"	Kritika	2	2	10	8
Gulika	19 Ar 27' 58.34"	Bharni	2	1	6	2
MAN	03Leo35	Magha	2	5	2	5

Rasi

```
+--------------------------------------+
|\            / \            /|
| \    Ke    /   \   GL     / |
|  \        /     \        /  |
|AL \ 12 /   AL   \ 10 /      |
|    \ /            \ /       |
| 1   x      As      x   9    |
|    / \            / \       |
| Gk /   \        /   \       |
|   /     \      /     \      |
|  /       \ 11 /       \     |
| /   Md    \ /          \    |
|   2        x     HL         |
|\          / \            /  |
| \        /   \     8    /   |
|  \      /     \        /    |
|   \    /   Sa  \      /     |
|Ju  \  /         \    /      |
|Su Me x  Ma        x   Mo    |
|     / \          / \        |
| 3  /   \  5     /   \  7    |
|   /     \      /     \      |
|  / Ve   \    /   Ra   \     |
| / 4      \ /     6     \    |
+--------------------------------------+
```

The native run away from home and his family members-wife does not know about him whether live or dead. The native came to me when he was indebted with Rs30/- lacks in February-2010. Recently in June--2013, he was indebted to 1.50 to 2.00 crores and ran away from home. 8H/3H share future trading, 7H general commerce, 6H indebtedness, 2H saved monies, 9H/5H house of fate/wealth. Karaka is Jupiter. When all these are afflicted, the native will be indebtedness heavily may be throughout life according to the predominance degree of affliction.

[01] MAN with orbs, one more element of affliction and Karaka element
Taking -4.30 dg orbs of Mars, we will get most afflicted degree at 3Leo35, Magha Nakstra – 2 by Mars & Saturn. Nakstra lord is Ketu and D9 lord is Venus of Taurus. Nakstra lord afflict 2H of saved liquidities with Rahu-Mars. 7H where Leo sign posited with Saturn - Mars amidst the house may destroy the business as dire malefic being 12HL & 3HL. Taurs the D9 sign is posited by Mandi, is aspected by Saturn-Rahu and its lord Venus in Saturn star and its lord is with rahu; thus the Venus combo is in 6-7-8 H indicating chronic debts or miserable end. In D9 Taurus sign is betwixt Rahu-Saturn-Mars in debts house 6th, its lord Venus discomforted aspected by Rahu. Venus is in cruel D60 portion karala damstra.

[02] Higher Division
Gulika, Sun, Mars, nodes and Saturn, heavily afflicts Taurs sign in D40. 3Leo35 dg means Leo sign of D40 afflicted by Saturn-Mars.

[03] Exception
Jupiter the kraka of money and wealth is in good position, Pushkar amsha, but its avstha is not good being old, asleep, distressed. How it helps is to be seen but the reality is that the native met with disastrous end as of now. Venus avastha is also not good being old, asleep and sad.

[04] Dasa system

V dasa at mid June – 2013 is Jupiter MD – Jupiter AD – Saturn PD the dasa lords are afflicted by natal and transit Rahu-Mars also to cause the huge indebtedness.

[05] Past life cursed karma & its expiation

The native was Brahman in manes world in India in Bihar like region. He was as a culprit and devoid of standard of life. One day his friend merchant came to him with lots of wealth and family. Brahman planned conspiracy, looted the merchant, and deserted his friend and family. The friend died facing penury and cursed the native.

For the expiation of this sinful karma do the laxmi vrata of Hindu lunar month 'Bhadrapada' day is 'shukla astmai' for 16-days. Do appropriate donation, charities and devotional service.

Chapter- 18

Most Afflicted Purvafalguni Nakstra

Male - HmnsuHbhgda
Date: December 3, 1985; Time: 23:05:00; Time Zone: 5:30:00 (East of GMT); Place:72 E 56' 00", 20 N 38' 00"; Valsad, India; Altitude: 0.00 meters; Ayanamsa: 22-12-51.
[Broader sense and Raman Aynamsa taken]

Rasi D1 Chart

```
+--------------------------------------+
| \          /     \     Mo    /  |
|    \ 6       /        \         /    |
|      \     /            \  4  /      |
| ke     \  /                \  /  3    |
|Ma      x         As          x  Md |
|  7      /  \               /  \      |
|      /      \            /      \     |
|    /          \        /          \    |
|  / MeR      \  5  /              \  |
| /     8           \  /                \ |
|  Sa  Su           x    2  Gk       |
| \                 /  \               / |
|   \     Ve     /      \             /  |
|     \         /          \         /    |
|       \     /              \     /      |
|         \  /                 \  /       |
|  9       x         AL       x    Ra |
|         /  \                 /  \       |
|       /      \     11     /      \    |
|     /          \          /          \  |
|   /      Ju      \     /     HL    \  |
| /        10        \  /    GL   12 \ |
+--------------------------------------+
```

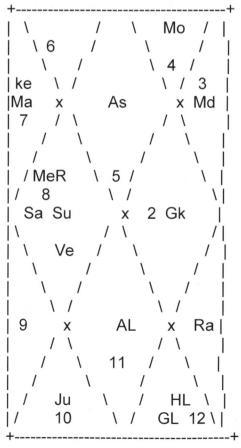

Body	Longitude	Star	Quart er	D1	D9	D60
Ascendant	0 Le 01' 24.29"	Magh	1	5	1	1
Sun	19Sc17'50.99"	Jyestha	1	8	9	8
Moon	29Cn17'34.65"	Aslesha	4	4	12	10
Mars	0 Li 57' 00.02"	Chitra	3	7	7	2
Mercury-R	8 Sc 37' 34.19"	Anuradha	2	8	6	6
Jupiter	20 Cp 34' 58.92"	Sravan	4	10	4	10
Venus	8 Sc 02' 27.42"	Anuradha	2	8	6	5
Saturn	9 Sc 46' 24.01"	Anuradha	2	8	6	8
Rahu	16 Ar 27' 25.29"	Bharani	1	1	5	10
Ketu	16 Li 27' 25.29"	Swati	3	7	11	10
Mandi	1 Ge 00' 57.90"	Mrigshirsa	3	3	7	2
Gulika	19 Ta 03' 57.84"	Rohini	3	2	3	8
MAN	14 Leo 46.24	PurvaFalguni	1	5	5	8

Died in the early beginning of 1/3-December-2013 for renal failure and other severe complications of lungs and blood; mother prepared to donate her kidney hospitalised, blood & kidney matched but the boy died. Kidney diseases proteins cannot hold weak functions near to renal failure suffered for about 20 years.

[01] MAN with orbs, one more element of affliction and Karaka element
Saturn at 09.46.24 dg in Scorpio and Rahu at 16.27.25 dg in Aries spoil Purvafalguni-1 nakstra by their aspect at 14.46.24 dg Leo if we consider +5.00 dg orbs for

Saturn and around -01.41 dg for Rahu [out of orbs range of 4.00 to 5.00 dg]. Navamsa sign is Leo and its lord is Sun. Leo sign is 1H & Sun both represents physique-soul, afflicted by Saturn, and Rahu is weak. Saturn is the lord of 6th afflicting Sun may cause disease and being with Venus may cause genetic defects also. MAN lord Venus in Saturn [7H] star both represents Kidney here. Some astrologers see Scorpio sign for kidney and urine drainage disease. And drainage lord Moon in acute gnadnta. The combination of Sun-Saturn-Venus is in Scorpio. Venus our MAN lord sign in D1 is Libra represents kidney is polluted by Mars-Ketu and limb karaka Jupiter weak enhance the kidney disease. Venus the seminal fluid holder looses the war to Mercury; Venus is in Kala, the cruel D60 degree portion. Sun is in D1 & D9 afflicted by Saturn and Rahu respectively. Sun and Jupiter is having lowest shadabala and Venus in Vriddha Avastha causing the blow. Karaka of kidney is Venus and Libra sign. Venus-Sun our MAN lord & its D9 lord afflicted by Saturn-Rahu respectively in D9. Swati-4 and Vishakha-4 nakstra ruled the kidney and urinary tract and when this are afflicted the disease caused. Here Saturn and Ketu / Rahu afflict it if we take broader sense of orbs. Some takes Chitra nakstra of Libra for kidney.

[02] Higher Division

The disease confirmed in D40. 14.46 dg of Leo sign means Scorpio sign in D40. Some astrologers see Scorpio sign for kidney and urine drainage disease. This sign, our MAN D9 lord and Venus all afflicted by Saturn the disease inflector. Mars aspect on Saturn-Sun there with Gulika may confirm the acute and dreadful kidney disease.

[03] Dasa system

Kala Chakra Dasa is applicable here at the time death; December-2013.
Cancer MD _ Libra AD Libra 3rd house is of premature death being 8th from 8th. Moon karaka of urine drainage in acute Ganadnta, will give the result of 1H, the life, and will come under the aspect of Saturn and Rahu [dim]. Venus the kidney karaka and holder of proteins heavily afflicted in Scorpio sign as MAN lord with MAN d9 lord Sun afflicted by Saturn.
In transit see that dire malefic Saturn-nodes are in 12th and 6th to Scorpio where natal Venus-Sun posited. Moon is aspected by transit Saturn.

[04] Exception
I do not see there is any exception available and life of the native is depended due to disease throughout.

[05] SCD
The death came in 28th year represent 4H. 4HL Mars is 12th to it in Libra being 3rd the premature death. Mars is with ketu the 'moxa' karaka.

[06] Past life cursed karma and its expiation [see chapter-5]
In previous life the native was a warrior, one day came to thick jungle. He killed in the way quadruplicate for food and consumed wine [Somarasa]. Roaming here and there, he saw a pond of pure water, nearby it one

agnihotra Guru Brahman [Brahman engaged to maintain & retain sacred fire]. Some female disciples were giving oblation to that Guru. By accident, the warrior saw one female disciple and was engrossed with sex. With that force, being drunk, perturbed limbs he fell down on her, he felt fall his seminal fluid, polluted the disciple. The female disciple gave him curse to suffer for lifetime and died in the wheel of time. The warrior also died in pilgrimage land after many years. In current era he consumed the cursed karma for the sinful karma and killing of quadruplicate.

For expiation of cursed karma of the native, do samputit japa of roganashana mantra with Saptasati chandi pataha and rudra patha for eleven times. Also do puruscharana of Shapa Nashna mantra. Do appropriate donation and devotional service to needy couple or donate on marriage ceremony of needy couple.

Japa and sacrifices be self-done. Appropriate donations, charity and devotional services should be given predominance, everywhere it is mentioned.

[The native died but for other such similar cases one may suggest this kind of expiation]

Chapter – 19

MA Dhanista Nakstra [Briefly explained]

Male -BhupsBhrti

Date: February 10, 1964; Time:17:10:00 pm; Time Zone: 5:30:00 (East of GMT); Place: 72 E 56' 00", 20 N 38' 00" Valsad, India; Ayanamsa: 23-20-25.69

```
Rasi
+-----------------------------------------------+
|\          / \ Md  Gk    / |
| \  5     /   \   Ra    /  |
|  \      /     \       /   |
|   \    /       \3    /    |
|    \ /         \ /       |
|6     x     As     x  AL |
|     / \         / \2      |
|    /   \       /   \      |
|   /     \     /     \     |
|  /       \ 4 /       \    |
| /   7     \ /         \   |
|            x     1         |
|\          / \          /  |
| \        /   \        /12|
|  \      / 10  \      /    |
|   \    /  Ma   \ /  Ju |
|    \ /          \/         |
|HL      x     Su       x Ve |
|     / \         / \       |
|8   /   \ Me    /   \      |
|   /     \     / 11  \     |
|  /  Mo   \ /  Sa     \    |
|/  Ke  9   \/  GL      \|
+-------------------------------------+
```

Body	Longitude	Star	Pada	D1	D9	D60
Ascendant	9 Cn 33' 49.10"	Pushya	2	4	6	11
Sun	27 Cp 26' 09.15"	Dhanista	2	10	6	4
Moon	21 Sg 36' 31.22"	PShadha	3	9	7	4
Mars	28 Cp 54' 16.54"	Dhanista	2	10	6	7
Mercury	6 Cp 05' 34.04"	UShadha	3	10	11	10
Jupiter	23 Pi 05' 41.00"	Revti	2	12	10	10
Venus	6 Pi 11' 56.17"	Ubhadra	1	12	5	12
Saturn	1 Aq 40' 51.43"	Dhanista	3	11	7	2
Rahu	17 Ge 23' 20.49"	Ardra	4	3	12	1
Ketu	17 Sg 23' 20.49"	PShadha	2	9	6	7
Mandi	10 Ge 25' 45.79"	Ardra	2	3	10	11
Gulika	0 Ge 41' 23.97"	Mrigshirsha	3	3	7	4
MAN	27 Cp40	Dhanista	2	10	6	

Dhanista-2 is the most afflicted nakstra by Sun-Mars-Saturn at 27.40 dg, taking orbs of Saturn at -4.00 dg. Nakstra lord is Mars and D9 sign is Virgo lord Mercury. Mercury being MAN D9 lord as 12HL & 3HL is a separator in 7H in paapkartari. Nakstra lord and sign lord Mars-Saturn both are combust. Broadly speaking Mercury is afflicted by Sun-Mars-Saturn in 7H and 7HL Saturn by Rahu in 8H of marital bond; all these planets are separatists mainly caused the native 'spouseless'. Mercury being afflicted and arudha of 11H is involved, Mars atmakaraka. Mercury affliction indicates matul shaapa. The soul involved in betrayal of spouse love and her use to fulfil the ambition caused personal sufferings to her in past life. Mercury is in cruel karaldamstra D60 part, Shadbal 97% only, Vridhha avastha, and dreaming, crippled and mischievous mood. Involvement of Arthatrikona 2H & 10H indicates sufferings due to money matters. In D9 Virgo our MAN D9 sign is heavily afflicted with 6/8 youga to its lord Mercury. Karaka element Venus exalted and Jupiter in own sign is the protector but weak in D9 and Shadabala & avastha.

In D60 Mercury is afflicted by Mars & Sun posited in Capricorn our D1 most afflicted sign with debilitated Jupiter.

Exception is Venus in vaiseshikams 'Devlokamsha' but is in cruel D60 part and its avastha is not helping.

The native is unmarried until the date so the dasa system is not envisaged.

The native in past live abide in a region of non-Hindus. He was devoid of his Brahman karma and was culprit, gossiping and conspiring to loot the people around him. He married to a Brahman woman but did not give the due respect and status to her as wife, looted her and deserted her. He thus comprehended wealth, diamonds and gold. He was also involved in human trafficking and abuse virgins. Due to this cursed karma the native is unmarried till the date.

For expiation feed needy/ starving couples. For its appeasing suitable-proper charity-donations-devotional, service to class of people or live being is to be done. Contribute to marriage ceremony of needy couple or share some expenses on marriage or education of girls. Help girls and married woman settling their rights.

Chapter -20

MA Revati Nakshtra

Female - SnlDsi

Date: March 23, 1968; Time: 17:10:00 pm; Time Zone: 5:30:00 (East of GMT) ; Place: 72 E 56' 00", 20 N 38' 00" Valsad, India; Ayanamsa: 23-23-52.41

Joint Arthritis – May-1984 first hospitalised at the age of 17th year running. Seven surgeries made, both knee disc replaced, hips replaced both, thigh fractured and operated. I have been seeing the native since last 20 years. Naturally, she is unmarried. Still she is walking and doing routine difficultly with support or otherwise bedridden. The entire life of the native is miserable and dependable.

Joint Rheumatoid Arthritis [RA] astrological factors -

Weak windy planets Moon, Saturn, Mercury and Venus i.e. combusted, afflicted, badly situated, conjoined with duhasthana lord especially 6th house of disease

Ketu also rules over windy disease

Ascendant lord, Sun, Moon weak

3H rules over rheumatoid disease; so the Gemin and Mercury govern this disease as natural zodiac sign. Aswini, Ardra, Punarvasu, Uttra-falguni, Hasta, Jyestha, Moola, Satabhisa and Puvra-bhadrapada are the stars ruling windy element and their affliction in ascendant, Sun, Moon etc may vitiate the body.

In this chart ascendant lord Sun with Rahu-Saturn-Gulika/Mandi in 8H from Ascendant is not at all good position and indicates widowhood or such similar condition. The native has to suffer for lifetime if confirmed. There is nothing fruitful in the chart.

Rasi

```
+-------------------------------------------+
|\          / \           / |
| \   Ke   /   \   4    /  |
|  \      /     \      /   |
|   \ 6  /Ju[R]  \    /    |
|    \ /          \ /     |
|AL    x    As     x  3   |
| 7   / \         / \     |
|    /   \       /   \    |
|   /     \     /     \   |
|  /       \ 5 /       \  |
| /         \ /         \ |
|      8      x     GL    |
| \         / \         / |
|  \       /   \  2    /  |
|   \     /     \     /   |
|    \   /  Ve   \   /    |
|     \ /         \ /     |
|      x    Me     x  Ma  |
| 9   / \         / \     |
|    /   \       /12  \ 1 |
|   /  10  \ 11 / Md \    |
|  /   Mo   \  /  Su  \   |
| /   HL     \ /Sa Ra Gk\  |
+-------------------------------------------+
```

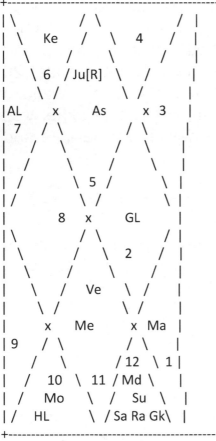

Body	Longitude	Star	Pad	Rasi	D9	D40
Lagna	16 Le 57' 33.46"	P Falguni	2	5	6	11
Sun - MK	9 Pi 30' 58.01"	U.Bhadra	2	12	6	7
Moon – PiK	5 Cp 08' 57.17"	U.Shada	3	10	11	1
Mars - DK	3 Ar 16' 58.12"	Asvini	1	1	1	5
Mercury – BK	14 Aq 05' 51.13"	Satatarka	3	11	11	7
Jupiter (R)	3 Le 45' 12.26"	Magha	2	5	2	6
Venus – AmK	16 Aq 22' 44.33"	Satatarka	3	11	11	10
Saturn – AK	20 Pi 23' 21.13"	Revati	2	12	10	10
Rahu – PK	25 Pi 24' 49.65"	Revati	3	12	11	4
Ketu	25 Vi 24' 49.65"	Chitra	2	6	5	4
Maandi	23 Pi 43' 09.95"	Revati	3	12	11	2
Gulika	9 Pi 04' 52.02"	U.Bhadra	2	12	6	7
MAN 25.23	25 Pi 23	Revti	3	12	11	4

[01] MAN with orbs, one more element of affliction and Karaka element

Taking Saturn orbs at +5.00 dg we find that Revti-3 is most afflicted at 25.23 dg by Saturn, Mandi and Rahu. MAN lord is Mercury and its D9 lord is Saturn, sign Aquarius. Sun with Gulika, Satrun and Rahu in 8H itself indicates that the native was born with innate defect. Soul is carrying the burden of prenatal karma; see Saturn being our MAN D9 lord. This may be spell as curse of Pitrus in preta-pisaach avastha causing this long term / lifetime sufferings of joints RA. Mercury our MAN lord in Satbhisha naktra of Saturn sign aspected by Jupiter-Venus but are 64th D9 lord from ascendant-Moon, is initiating cause of RA. Now see D9 chart where Aquarius sign our MAN D9 sign is posited by all windy planets Moon, Venus and Mercy affected by nodal axis in 6/12 house is the root cause of disease and long term sufferings. Karaka of RA is Mercury and Gemini sign in D9 aspected by Rahu.

The combination in 8H indicates that there is nothing fruitful in the chart except longevity.

[02] Higher Division
25.23 dg of Pisces means Cancer sign in D40, afflicted by nodes and Saturn. Saturn the lord of ascendant of D40 and our MAN D9 lord is in 12th house of hospitalisation and medical expenditure. Mercury the karaka of RA is with Gulika and debilitated Sun. Heavily afflicted Cancer sign is 8th to Arudha Lagna of D40 also indicates nija dosha soul carrying from prenatal adobe.
[03] Dasa system
The native when first hospitalised early May-1984 is the triggering time we may take and then series of sufferings and surgeries are made and the native faces long term trauma.
Kala Chakra Dasa is applicable here.
Taurus MD_ Pisces AD
Taurus lord is posited in our MAN D9 sign with MAN lord Mercury in 7H of Maraka. Venus is the lord of 3H also being 8th to 8th as per 'भावात् भावम्... bhāvāt bhāvam' rule in 7H became acute maraka. Pisces lord is Jupiter in exchange to Sun posited in 6/8 yoga aspecting Venus in our MAN D9 sign and MAN lord Mercury. This entire dasa gamut is played in the house no. 1-8-7 indicating chronic trouble to the life of the native due to past life karma.
This dasa sign/lord in transit is afflicted by dire malefic. See Taurus sign and its lord Venus is aspected by transit Mars-Rahu and Pisces sign is in 6/8 yoga to transit Saturn.
Natrual karaka of this disease Mercury-Gemini and 3H/3HL are afflicted in *toto in* transit in the event month.
[04] Exception
Sun in pushkar amsha, Jupiter-Venus-Mercury as natural benefice in Kendra, another life giving Mars in

own sign helps the native give desire to live at all time in spite of this death like sufferings. In D40 Jupiter aspcting our MAN D9 lord Saturn and Venus with it give the life boost.

[05] Past Life Karma and its expiation

In prenatal adobe, the native was a beautiful looking wife of salt miner, master of sacred scriptures, eloquent, wide and held in high esteem by royals. However, she is culprit, bad and adulterous. One-day, a Brahmin friend of the salt miner came to him from too far place. Brahman is with lots of wealth and ornaments with him. Brahman was to settle in nearby places and came alone. He resides for a moth there. The couple humbly respect him and gives him warm welcome. The wife of salt-miner conspiring and try hard to indulge the Brahman to commit adultery, but vitreous he denied the same. However, she again tried and succeeded. One day she gives poison in the supper of the Brahman and when dead, throw his body in the flowing river. She takes all the wealth and ornaments and consumes them and in the time wheel died and came again to current era to consume her sins. Due to this conspired and secret sin of the past life the woman suffered for lifetime and those who helped her in prenatal adobe now are his Brother doing all kind of medical expenditure and support for her.

Expiation of this is not easy. Puruscharana of sataxari Gayatri mantra is required for three times. Does sacrifice in the regular vagina type 'havana kunda'. Feed needy/ starving couples. For its appeasing suitable-proper charity-donations-devotional, service to class of people or live being is to be done. By doing, this without doubt physical well-being is gained or minimized.

Note- Sataxari Gayatri mantra is a mantra with 100 syllables comprises gayatri mantra, tryambaka mantra and savitri mantra. Puruschanran is japa, Havana, tarpana, marajana and bhojana as per ritual performance customs. Japa required doing in Brahma Muhurat [early morning 3.00 to 4.00 AM as per night hours]

Chamar Yoga [JP-Subramanyam Sashtri CH-7 V136/137] is formed in two type when two benefice occupied 1H, 7H, 9H or 10H [here in the chart it is Mercury-Venus in 7H] ; when lagna lord occupying the exaltation sign and aspected by Jupiter be in Kendra [Jupiter-Sun in exchange] the resulting yoga is called Chamara yoga. Here this yoga is broken by two reason of ascendant lord Sun and Saturn the depositor of 7HL where Venus-Mercury posited are in 8H with nodal excel and Gulika. Ascendant lord Sun and Jupiter is in exchange in 6/8 yoga in 1/8 house axis.

Auspicious results of this yoga are destroyed due to past life karma. She is beautiful looking female master of sacred scriptures, eloquent, wide and held in high esteem by royals.

However, she is not good looking, she could not study well; she is neither eloquent nor intelligent and she is unmarried. Due to bad karma of past life, she has to suffer for lifetime.